# The Quest for Indiana University Football Glory

INDIANA UNIVERSITY PRESS

# The Quest for Indiana University Football Glory

## Pete DiPrimio

This book is a publication of

INDIANA UNIVERSITY PRESS
Office of Scholarly Publishing
Herman B Wells Library 350
1320 East 10th Street
Bloomington, Indiana 47405 USA

iupress.indiana.edu

© 2019 by Pete DiPrimio

*Manufactured in the United States of
America*

Cataloging information is available from
the Library of Congress.

ISBN 978-0-253-03458-8 (paperback)
ISBN 978-0-253-03459-5 (ebook)

1  2  3  4  5  23  22  21  20  19

# Contents

*Images follow page 36*

# Acknowledgments

THIS BOOK WOULDN'T HAVE BEEN POSSIBLE WITHOUT help from caring, passionate, and knowledgeable people. I want to thank IU senior assistant athletic director Jeff Keag, who came up with this idea and who was *always* there when I needed help and guidance, which happened often. Assistant athletic director Greg Kinkaid was also a huge help on so many levels.

I want to thank IU football coach Tom Allen for allowing amazing access and for showing kindness and courtesy at every step. The same goes for Tom's wife, Tracy; son, Thomas; and parents, Tom Sr. and Janet. They were very gracious and accommodating.

A big thanks to all the Hoosier coaches and staff members, who were always friendly and made me feel welcome and comfortable, even when I got in the way.

Also thanks to former Indianapolis Ben Davis High School coach Dick Dullaghan; the late Bill Mallory, the former IU football coach who passed away in the summer of 2018; Hall of Fame radio announcer Don Fischer; Hall of Fame sports writer Bob Hammel; ex–IU All-America football player Ken Kaczmarek; former standout Hoosier wide receiver Eric Stolberg; former Indiana head coach Lee Corso; athletic director Fred Glass; senior associate athletic director Jeremy Gray; Bloomington (Ind.) St. Charles Borromeo Catholic School teacher and fellow fitness instructor Maria Hamilton for her invaluable proofreading; and so many more who took time to help during the course of this project.

Another big, special thanks to IU Director of Strategic Communications John Decker, who came in to help with the photos. If it weren't for him, there is no way this book would have gotten finished by the deadline.

In other words, it's time for a really big, manly hug.

Thanks also to Ashley Runyon and the IU Press staff for all their help and patience. Heaven knows I needed it.

Finally, thanks to my family: wife Cindy, daughter Gabrielle, son Vince, and, of course, Rocky the super dog.

# The Quest for Indiana University Football Glory

# Introduction

TOM ALLEN JOGS INTO A BRISK NOVEMBER WIND SWIRLING around Memorial Stadium. A red-and-white Indiana University ball cap is wedged low on his forehead, covering short brown hair sprinkled near his ears with the beginning of gray. His square-jawed face, capable of room-warming smiles or player-jolting glares, depending on the situation, shows no emotion.

Glasses give him a scholarly appearance, a hint of the accountant he once thought he would be and the preacher he might one day become—when the coaching ends.

It is just before noon on a cold, partly sunny day, and Indiana's football coach squeezes in a run between morning practice and early-afternoon meetings.

He is a solidly built man who still looks capable of tackling a running back on the football field or pinning an opponent on a wrestling mat.

He once did both.

Those days are decades in his past, but the passion and drive that once led to athletic success remain.

Purdue is on his mind. The annual Old Oaken Bucket Game looms in a few days, with a 2017 bowl reward going to the winner. A potential breakthrough season has been stymied by a series of heartbreaking losses and frustrating injuries, but a winning record is possible with a victory over the Boilers and then in a bowl game.

Allen runs alone, but he is not alone. He has surrounded himself with good people, quality people, people who care as much as he does about the players, the program, and the university.

He was hired to deliver consistent winning in the manner of former Hoosier coaching great Bill Mallory, and the challenge is steep—the brutal reality of a Big Ten East schedule with a program that has had just one winning record since 1994—because it always is at Indiana.

Allen has the resources, facilities, and commitment to succeed. He has won at every place he has worked, from high school to college, large schools and small, and it has led to this cream 'n' crimson opportunity.

So he runs and thinks and plans.

Potential victory is out there, as it has been for so many Hoosier coaches who have ended up, like Tantalus in Greek mythology, forever reaching for fruit they can't grasp and water they can't drink.

Can Allen reach and drink it?

Can Hoosier glory—and there are encouraging flashes of that in the forever-struggling program's more than a century of existence—be found again?

Answers lie in faith, belief, effort, recruiting, and the cornerstone of Allen's program:

L-E-O.

Love Each Other.

⊷⇒ ⇐⊶

When the clock strikes midnight, Tracy Allen knows she can talk to her husband. That's usually when Tom Allen is most likely to be at home.

"That's our time to talk," she says, "because he works eighteen-hour days."

Otherwise, Allen is at Memorial Stadium or on the recruiting trail or off doing something to help deliver a winner. It's a 6:00-a.m.-to-midnight-and-beyond world that works because, most of all, it's a labor of love.

"It's important to have a passion," Tracy says. "Tom is passionate about his job. He's a high-energy guy. He doesn't need much sleep."

Indiana football has a way of limiting sleep time. It's an often unforgiving challenge that only the toughest of coaches can overcome. Tracy believes her husband is tough enough. She calls him the Lion Chaser, and it is not a cute nickname people sometimes give loved ones.

It comes from the Bible, from Joshua 1:9, and it says, "Have I not commanded you? Be strong and courageous. Do not be afraid; do not be discouraged, for the LORD your God will be with you wherever you go."

A framed photo of a lion is in Allen's Memorial Stadium office as a reminder.

Allen is the latest cream 'n' crimson coach to tackle what so often is the unbeatable foe, and if he didn't understand that before his 2017 debut season as head coach, he certainly did after.

The hoped-for breakthrough didn't happen in his IU head coaching debut. A 5–7 record ended two straight seasons of bowl-making opportunity.

You'd better believe it stung.

A second 5–7 record in 2018 doubled the sting.

No matter. Allen, forty-eight years old in the fall of 2018, keeps pushing with the energy of a man half his age. He doesn't know any other way.

Sometimes team mascots pay the price.

Several years ago, when Allen was coaching at Mississippi, the Rebels were playing at Louisiana State, where few visiting teams win. Mississippi was leading at halftime. Allen was so excited that he tackled the Mississippi mascot. Allen's son, Thomas, was there to watch and wonder.

"I was like, 'Dad, what are you doing?' He jumps up smiling. That's kind of the guy he is. He's crazy. He's psycho. He can't hit his players, so he'd hit me for the fun of it."

For the record, these were not the kind of hits to generate parental abuse concerns, but they were hard enough to annoy.

"I was like, 'OK, I'm not going to stand by you anymore,'" Thomas says. "But I enjoyed every minute of it. He's all fire. He's fun to be around and to be a player for."

Thomas should know. He turned down other scholarship offers to join the IU program as a linebacker for the start of the 2017 season.

"He's one of the great defensive minds," the son says. "He loves his players. He gets his players to play hard for him. That's why I came here—who would I play harder for, some random guy or my father?

"He makes players—some he recruited, some he didn't—play harder than they've ever played before. At the end of the day, that's how you win."

Allen is a passionate coach, a caring coach, the kind of coach who demands without demeaning, who motivates without crossing lines.

Dick Dullaghan was as good a high school football coach as the state of Indiana has ever produced, with eight state titles and one national championship. As a mentor and friend to Allen, Dullaghan says all good coaches have the *it* factor. He insists Allen has it—and more.

"It comes in all shapes and sizes and forms," Dullaghan says. "He has it. He's going to get it done at Indiana.

"He's totally genuine. He says it like it is. He's honest but never profane or egotistical. He never attacks people. He attacks their effort and their belief in themselves. He challenges them. He does it in a manner that doesn't demean them."

Dullaghan calls it "loving them into submission."

"He works like it depends on him and prays like it depends on God," he says. "There is no phoniness or pretense. He's a guy who cares about his fellow man. He cares about changing the Indiana program.

"It's all there. It's all possible. There's no question in my mind.

"You can't win on a national scale without getting players from parts of the entire country. You can't just recruit Indiana.

You've got to recruit all over the country. If you don't, somebody else will.

"You have to have a program that is national in scope if you intend to compete for a Big Ten or national championships. Rome wasn't built in a day. It takes time. You need good players, treat them right, develop them, and keep your staff together.

"Players don't care how much you know until they know how much you care. When they know you do care, they give you more than you imagined. They put it all out there. They don't want to let you down.

"To get players to play hard, you have to love them into submission."

And then . . .

"I respect him so much," Dullaghan says. "I never doubted that he would be successful."

Allen connects to IU's football past, to the glory days of Bill Mallory and the unshakable optimism of Terry Hoeppner, to the improbable 1967 Rose Bowl run, the dominating 1945 Big Ten championship, and the zany Holiday Bowl victory under Lee Corso.

Is this his dream job?

"When I think about being in your home state, being able to be in the Big Ten, and being able to lead *the* Indiana University, it's pretty special," Allen says.

"I'm cautious because I can't say I dreamed of this my whole life. You never know how things will play out. I never thought I would be at Ole Miss. I never thought I'd be at South Florida. You never know where your path is going to lead.

"The opportunity to be here is a dream come true."

Hoeppner's legacy—he died of brain cancer in 2007, just a couple of years after getting the Hoosier head coaching job—resonates strongly with Allen.

"My favorite tradition at Indiana is when we come out and all the players touch Hep's Rock before they take the field," he says.

"I knew him personally. He was a friend of my family, and we were friends of his family. He was a special, special person. A special coach. He was obviously doing great things at Indiana till his life was cut short, tragically. He'll always be a special part of what we do at Indiana."

Indiana has won before, most consistently under Mallory, and, Allen insists, will win again. Dullaghan backs him up.

"I don't know how soon," he says, "but they will win a Big Ten championship. It's going to happen."

Understanding how starts with unprecedented access to that 2017 debut season, and beyond.

So it begins again.

## CHAPTER 1

# Passion Play

TOM ALLEN STORMS INTO THE MEMORIAL STADIUM locker room. He charges in like a bull, a bear, like the former standout football player and wrestler he once was. Emotion coils like a spring waiting to snap.

"Everybody get in here!" he shouts with a hoarse voice, as if sandpaper had raked across his vocal cords.

This is no time for subtlety or calm. There is a football culture to change, a losing tradition to smash, heartbreaking loss to overcome, and another chance to find words to do what actions couldn't.

Players gather and bend knees. The air is heavy with sweat and passion. A mid-October 2017 homecoming game against No. 17 Michigan that could have been won was not. Another opportunity is lost, but another waits. In a week, Indiana will head to No. 18 Michigan State; Allen needs his Hoosiers ready, and it starts with this postgame speech and this thought: adversity is not the enemy.

"Fire exposes," Allen has said previously. "It reveals. That's why you want the fire. You don't want too much adversity, but as a coach, you know it'll help you grow."

The Hoosiers need growth, and Allen was hired to develop it. It's his first season as a college head coach, and the mission is clear—shatter a losing Hoosier football tradition that has stretched on for a decade, that has, in truth, stretched on for a generation of decades. He's here to do what so many coaches couldn't.

So Allen pushes for perspective and inspiration amid locker room disappointment.

"I want you to listen, and listen clear!" he shouts to his kneeling players. "This ain't about breakthrough. This ain't about falling short again. It's about fighting your tails off and giving it everything you've got and just coming up short. That's what this is about!"

Players listen intently, motionless as statues.

"You don't hang your head," Allen says. "You don't throw yourself around. You don't make excuses. You fought, and you fought, and you fought! And I'm proud of you."

Allen pauses and paces. He isn't here to tear down or to coddle. It's a tough world and a tough sport, and nobody gives you anything. You earn your breaks.

"You didn't think, *Here we go again.* That's bull crap! That's losing mentality! You played a good football team. We had our opportunities, didn't we?"

"Yes, sir," players say in unison.

"Yes, we did. It hurts. It ought to hurt. People can say, 'If I was you, I'd hang my head.' Nobody did that. I love this team!

"If [critics] come at us, it's on me. I'll take it all. I'll take all their bullets. I'll take all their arrows. I believe in you. You played so hard. You fought to the end.

"I don't want to hear nothing but positives. Do you understand me?"

"Yes, sir!"

Allen is tired of it; everybody wearing cream 'n' crimson is—tired of the pushing, working, planning, and striving so that you get to the brink of the mountaintop but not the summit. You give everything you've got, again and again, and watch others celebrate.

On this sun-splashed October day, warm as June despite the calendar, sixty minutes of football wasn't enough. Indiana had overcome Michigan, its own mistakes, perceived officiating flaws, and as good a defense as there was in college football. It had forced improbable overtime, scoring ten points in the final three and a half minutes against a defense that hadn't allowed a fourth-quarter point all season.

It wasn't enough.

In overtime, IU had Michigan tailback Karan Higdon stopped for a three-yard loss, only to see him break free for a touchdown. Then the Hoosiers had first and goal at the 2-yard line and couldn't score the tying touchdown.

It came down to makeable plays that weren't made, but Allen was compelled to address the unspoken perspective.

"You ain't getting no breaks. Don't expect it. You ain't getting nothing! I don't care. It's not an excuse. We've got to earn the right to get those breaks. That's the truth. I'm just telling you. You got to earn that. We're not there yet. I don't care."

A pause.

"I love this team."

Another pause. Homecoming weekend brings off-the-field temptations, and postgame trouble is one bad decision away. Allen and his staff are not babysitters. He treats players as men and hopes they act accordingly.

"Do the right thing tonight. You protect the team in all you do. We're going to go to battle again next week. I don't want anybody beside me but you and all these coaches. That's what I want. I love you. I appreciate you. I'll be behind you no matter what."

A final pause.

"Let's pray."

They bow their heads for the Lord's Prayer.

Tom Allen is a Christian man. He lives a life based on faith, belief, and unwavering enthusiasm. Few expected him to be here, including himself. He never envisioned being Indiana's head football coach. His goal was to be a Big Ten defensive coordinator, which he achieved in 2016 when then IU coach Kevin Wilson hired him.

Allen directed a remarkable one-year turnaround that saw the Hoosiers go from one of the nation's worst defenses to a top-fifty unit. That led to this Indiana head coaching opportunity and the drive for a "breakthrough season."

And why not? It was time to bring winning football back to Bloomington, to start a run of success last seen when Bill Mallory coached the program from the mid-1980s to the mid-1990s.

Everything was in place: quality players, experience, a talented and diverse coaching staff, impressive facilities, an exciting schedule, and more.

The only thing left was to win.

The Hoosiers didn't in 2017. Close games, winnable games, came down to one or two plays they did not make. The same thing happened in 2018.

But the sense is they will.

Soon.

A top-40-in-the-nation 2019 recruiting class, the best in program history, suggested the potential.

Why can Allen deliver when men such as Cam Cameron, Gerry DiNardo, Terry Hoeppner, Bill Lynch, and Kevin Wilson could not?

Let's take a look.

## CHAPTER 2

# Finding Perspective

TO UNDERSTAND THE CHALLENGE ALLEN FACES, AS SO many have faced before, means understanding that Indiana football history is dominated by coaches who tried and failed. Twenty-nine men have coached the Hoosiers since they first had a team in 1887, and six finished with winning records.

Five of those six coached before 1922.

In the last ninety-five years, only Bo McMillin wound up with more wins than losses. He went 63–48–11 with a 1945 Big Ten title from 1934 to '47. He was inducted into the College Football Hall of Fame in 1951. He's one of six Hoosiers to receive that honor.

No IU coach has ever had a winning Big Ten record. McMillin came the closest at 34–34–6.

As for that 1945 championship, it came as World War II was ending. The Hoosiers had shown promise the previous season by going 7–3.

Indiana opened with three straight road games. They won 13–7 at Michigan, tied 7–7 at Northwestern, and won 6–0 at Illinois. That started a roll that included a 7–2 win over No. 14 Tulsa, a 49–0 victory at No. 20 Minnesota, and a 26–0 victory at No. 19 Purdue.

The Hoosiers shut out their final three opponents and finished with 4 shutouts on the season, a record that still stood after the 2017 season. They led the Big Ten in scoring (27.9 points) and points allowed (5.6). They finished with a No. 4 national ranking. Unbeaten Army, Navy, and Alabama finished ahead of them in the national poll.

End Bob Ravensberg earned All-American honors, as did offensive lineman Russ Deal, two-way lineman Howard Brown, and freshman running back George Taliaferro, who led the conference with 719 rushing yards.

Taliaferro was the first African American to lead the Big Ten in rushing. He later punted for the Hoosiers, averaging 40.5 yards as a senior. That same 1948 season, he also threw for a team-leading 550 yards and 3 touchdowns as a quarterback. Taliaferro was inducted into the College Football Hall of Fame in 1981. In 1949, he became the first African American to be drafted by an NFL team—the Chicago Bears. He was a three-time Pro Bowl selection and finished with 2,266 rushing yards and 1,300 more as a receiver.

Ravensberg played two seasons in the NFL for the Chicago Cardinals. Deal was the IU team captain in 1945. Brown played two years in the NFL before becoming a long-time Hoosier football coach.

IU had two other players earn All-Big Ten recognition that season: end Ted Kluszewski and end/fullback Pete Pihos. The six-foot-two, 240-pound Kluszewski would go on to have a fifteen-year All-Star Major League baseball career, mostly with the Cincinnati Reds. Injuries limited his playing time, but he still hit .298 with 279 home runs and 1,028 runs batted in. In one four-year stretch, he hit 40, 49, 47, and 35 home runs while driving in more than 100 runs each season.

Pihos's IU career was interrupted by two years of military service during World War II. After setting school records for touchdowns, total points, and catches, he played eight seasons in the NFL for the Philadelphia Eagles. He made All-Pro six times and led the NFL in receptions for three straight years. He was inducted into the College Football Hall of Fame in 1966 and the Pro Football Hall of Fame in 1970.

As for Indiana football, it had two more good years under McMillin, going 6–3 in 1946, and finishing No. 20 in the national rankings, and 6–3 in 1947.

Then McMillin left to coach in the NFL, first with the Detroit Lions and then the Philadelphia Eagles, and losing became an unwanted Hoosier tradition for most of the next seventy years.

Can Tom Allen blast that losing away for a decade or more?

Former Hoosier All-American linebacker Ken Kaczmarek is optimistic. "I think he can get them into the Rose Bowl. He has a passion. He's very sincere. He knows how to build a team. He gets everybody on the same page, and getting young men on the same page is hard to do because there are so many distractions.

"When it gets down to it, you still have to play basic football. He has the right attitude. [In the 2017 season], we were probably three to four players away from going 8–4 or 9–3. And when you get to that point, then you can win it all.

"When Tom got the head coaching job, we talked. He said, 'I'm still going to be the defensive coordinator.' I said, 'Good.' That killed Brady Hoke at Michigan. They wouldn't let him do that. That was his forte. That makes me feel good.

"Tom said, 'I'm going to bring in a solid offensive coordinator so I don't have to do that.' I asked about special teams. He said, 'We'll emphasize that.'

"Mistakes happen during games. Somebody misses a block. Somebody throws an interception or fumbles.

"These are twenty-something-year-old kids. They do dumb things. You can only coach them. You can't lead them to water. Tom has the right attitude to bring us along."

To understand where Allen's attitude comes from and what it could produce means starting from the beginning.

## CHAPTER 3

# Allen in the Beginning

AS A CHILD, TOM ALLEN WAS NO SAINT. LET'S GET THAT out of the way right now. He was, says his father, Tom Sr., "a stinker."

"He got into a lot of trouble at home," the elder Allen says. "He had the rod of correction quite a few times."

His mother, Janet, offers a different perspective, as only a mother can.

"He was funny," she says.

The son grew up in a coaching world. Tom Sr. was a successful Indiana high school football coach at New Castle and elsewhere, and young Tom learned early the nuances and dedication the sport demanded. But before that, he learned more practical lessons, such as the "rod of correction."

Insight comes in a dark SUV parked in a Memorial Stadium parking lot on a brisk Saturday night. Tom Sr. and Janet have just returned from Indiana's 24–14 victory at Illinois—Allen's first win in Big Ten play. A drive to their New Castle–area home looms, but first come the stories. From the driver's seat, Tom Sr. talks in a soft voice.

He's two months removed from quadruple bypass surgery that caused him to miss a couple of his son's games, which is a big deal because he and his wife *never* miss home games.

Tom Sr. is back, watching walk-throughs and meetings, offering suggestions when asked and when not asked. Coaching nature is hard to turn off.

He and Janet had met in the small Indiana town of Morocco. Both came from large families. Tom Jr.'s dad had nine brothers and sisters. His mom had seven. Family had always mattered. So did doing things the right way.

The elder Allen considers the two sides of his son as a boy—rule breaker at home, rule follower away from it.

"In school," Tom Sr. says, "he became completely different. In our first [parent-teacher] session with the kindergarten teacher, we said he could be mischievous."

Janet leans forward from the backseat, set to soften whatever her husband says about her boy.

"He was busy," she says. "He had to be busy."

Tom Sr. smiles. "The teacher said, 'Oh, no. Not little Tommy. He's not mischievous. He's so sweet. He does everything we ask him. He gets along with the kids.' We never had trouble with him in school. He said funny things."

Janet nods in agreement. "He always made us laugh."

Actually, it wasn't always "always."

When Allen was around four years old, he decided to play a little hide-and-seek without his parents' knowledge or permission.

"I was coaching at Benton Central," Tom Sr. says, "and there were cornfields all around where we lived. One day, we couldn't find Tommy. We looked everywhere. We thought he got in the cornfield."

Adds Janet, "We were getting ready to go into the cornfield, and I said, 'Let's check the house one more time.'"

They'd already searched the house and found nothing. A second search paid off.

"I opened the door of a closet, and there he was, hiding," Janet says. "He had the biggest grin on his face."

She pauses. Motherly sweetness turns tough.

"You just wanted to beat him."

And then she did just that, and if this seems to violate today's don't-spank-a-child political correctness, well, back in the 1980s and before that, tough parenting, just like tough coaching, got results.

"I'd checked the closet before, so I don't know where he'd been before," Janet says. "I disciplined him. I paddled him."

Here's another story. There was a TV tower near the house. Tom Sr. set a rule: don't you dare climb the tower. For Tom and his brother, Nate, this was like telling a thirsty man not to drink. The temptation to climb was too great.

"The boys weren't allowed on it," Tom Sr. says. "One day, I go outside, and I see a neighbor grinning. I ask him what he's laughing at. I look up, and there my boys were on that tower. They had climbed up and were dropping files to see if they would stick in the ground.

"They both got in trouble for that."

Then comes one final story. Tom Sr. and his two sons were hiking along a nearby creek.

"Tommy picked up a rock and tried to throw it across the creek," Tom Sr. says. "Just as he threw it, Nate stood up and got hit on the head. Nate would act it out, so I don't know how badly he was hurt, but that upset me. I disciplined Tommy for that."

Tom Sr. smiles.

"That's why he obeys so well. He got so much correction."

Allen channeled all that energy into sports, becoming a successful multisport athlete in a time before specialization took hold. He earned nine letters in football, wrestling, and track at New Castle Chrysler High School. He was an all-state football player while playing for his father and a two-time wrestling state qualifier who finished fourth at state at 189 pounds as a senior. As a shot putter coached by his father, he won two sectionals and a regional. That was more than enough for Allen to eventually make the New Castle athletic hall of fame.

Allen went to Maranatha Baptist University in Wisconsin where he became a four-time all-conference linebacker as well as a National Christian College Athletic Association All-America wrestler for Olympic gold medalist Ben Peterson. In 1991, he won Maranatha Baptist's Ben Peterson Christian Sportsmanship Award in wrestling.

Allen also met this cute girl, Tracy, who would become his wife. Details to follow.

After college, Allen thought about becoming an accountant, but the urge to coach was too strong. This didn't surprise his parents.

"When he was growing up," Tom Sr. says, "we called him the Pied Piper because he seemed to have a knack to get kids to follow him."

That knack eventually led to coaching.

"He accepted it as a challenge," Tom Sr. says. "The more he learned, the more he got involved. He allowed himself to be pulled into coaching instead of being pushed into it."

For twelve years, Allen coached at the high school level at four different schools in Florida and Indiana. Then came a decade-long run as a college assistant coach before he took over the Hoosier program in December of 2016.

Did Mom and Dad ever see their son as a Big Ten head coach?

"Not really," Tom Sr. says. "I thought he might be a defensive coordinator."

As for what makes the younger Allen a successful coach, his father says, "He likes people. He has a real desire for people to do right and have great morals. I never heard him say a bad word except when he was coaching. He was at Arkansas State, and they were playing at Illinois. He got upset and said some bad words. I was like, 'Woo, I never heard him say that.'"

Coaching is tough on those who do it. It might be tougher on loved ones watching them do it.

"We go to the games," Janet says, "and I hate to say it, but it's not fun. You just want them to win. You want them to be successful. It's hard."

Adds Tom Sr.: "Sometimes I have to talk to myself. It's pretty stressful."

Janet nods in agreement.

"Oh, it's a lot more stressful with him as a coach than as a player. Oh, my, yes. Absolutely. He works so hard. You want him to get the fruits of his labor."

Tom Sr. thinks back to a few hours earlier and Indiana's win over Illinois.

"Maybe that will give them the confidence they need to keep winning," he says, and then his own coaching nature kicks in while thinking about quarterback Richard Lagow, who had just regained the starting job after an injury to Peyton Ramsey.

"I hope they make Richard realize he had a big part in this win. I'd just like to see him run straight ahead and slide. If I was six-six and 240 pounds like he is, I'd just run over tacklers. I don't know why he doesn't. He's bigger than those secondary kids. Just run over them." He chuckles. "I can say that because I'm not accountable."

The night grows late. It's time for Tom Sr. and Janet to start the drive home. One final thought comes about why their son has a chance to win at Indiana when so many others could not.

"Tom is very intense," Tom Sr. says and winks. "He gets that from his mother."

Janet smiles. "Tommy is intense—in a good way."

And then they drive off into the night.

## CHAPTER 4

# Allen's Early Coaching

IT WAS 1992; THE COACHING PROFESSION CALLED, AND Tom Allen knew what he was getting into. After all, he'd grown up with it. Tom Sr. set an example—as a father and as a coach—that became part of his son's DNA. Friday nights produced a special bond that still resonates.

"Friday night was the highlight of my whole week as a kid," Allen says. "My dad would come to our grade school and pick us up, my brother and I, and we'd go to the game. If it was an away game, we'd ride the bus.

"Everything to me about high school football was something I looked forward to as a kid, and then I got to high school and got to play for my dad."

In some ways, Allen still does.

"When I look at the way I live my life now, at the things I care about, it all started, really, with just how my father loved people," Allen says. "He genuinely loved his players, and they loved him back.

"He was very empathetic about their lives, and where they came from, and how he could relate to them well. And looking back, seeing how it wasn't just teaching young men how to play football but also how to value things, those were life lessons that my dad taught me."

Beyond that, Allen says, "My dad being a high school coach gave me a perspective on it. The character piece. And how you treat people. I saw that in him. How he had a tremendous heart for his people, how he cared about them. And about being honest. And how your word means something. The integrity of what you do. All the time.

"His consistency. You'd see it at home and in his role at school. How he was respected and was well thought of. In this profession, you're scrutinized for your behavior, on the field and off, and I was taught by him. It matters. You treat people as you'd like to be treated."

In other words, you treat them like family.

"My players are all my sons," Allen says. "And I treat them the way I'd want my son treated."

Allen's coaching odyssey didn't start in isolation. He married a woman who matched him in drive and success. He and Tracy met, as fate would have it, in the cafeteria at Maranatha Baptist in the late 1980s.

"It was in our freshman year," Tracy says. "He was a wrestler who was trying to lose weight after football season. We struck up a conversation about how he couldn't have ice cream. He had to have a salad. We chatted a little bit."

Eventually, they chatted a lot.

"I was very quiet," Tracy says. "It took me a while to talk to him. I was cautious. He's pretty focused. He knows what he wants."

Tracy grew up in Pennsylvania as a Penn State fan. She also was a good athlete who was a setter on the Maranatha volleyball team. She had an aunt who coached Shippensburg University of Pennsylvania to three national field hockey titles at the NCAA Division II level. Tracy and Tom dated for a couple of years, got engaged as juniors, and got married right out of college. Then the job search began.

"Tom sent out a ton of résumés," Tracy says. "He was a business teacher and taught accounting. I was a high school math teacher."

They found three schools that could accommodate their teaching preferences—one in North Carolina, one in South Carolina, and one in Florida. Tracy preferred either North or South Carolina, but Temple Heights High School in Florida was the only one with a football coaching opening.

"I remember asking him if coaching was that big of a deal. His answer was yes. So I said OK."

Tom coached football and wrestling. Tracy coached volleyball.

"We were young and without kids," Tracy says. "We worked eighteen-hour days. We painted the locker room. We drove the van. In his second year, he was the youngest head coach in the state of Florida."

After two years at Temple Heights, including a 7–4 record that produced the school's first-ever postseason appearance, they moved to Armwood High School in Florida. Allen was the defensive coordinator and helped Armwood go 8–2 and 10–2 in their two years there. By then they'd had their first child, Hannah. Brittany and Thomas would follow in the next four years.

Allen wanted to return to Indiana. While at Armwood, he took some of his best players to the highly regarded Bishop-Dullaghan football camp in Indianapolis during the summers. There he met Dick Dullaghan.

Dullaghan was the camp's driving force and one of the nation's most respected high school coaches. He'd go on to win more than three hundred games, eight state championships, and a national title during his time at Indianapolis Chatard, Carmel, and Ben Davis high schools.

"I watched him coach during our camp," Dullaghan says. "I watched his enthusiasm. He was an excellent teacher."

In 1997, Allen returned to Indiana and spent a year at Marion High School as the defensive coordinator under Mark Surface, who had once coached at New Castle. Tom Sr. had been one of his assistant coaches and then replaced him as the Trojan head coach. The younger Allen made instant defensive impact as Marion went 10–0 during the regular season.

"Marion hadn't had much success in the previous ten to fifteen years," Dullaghan says. "Tom was there just one year because I hired him the next year.

"It was obvious interviewing Tom that he was a special guy. He was good on his feet, very smart, a strong Christian man, and a great example for young people.

"Some coaches have this knack. Tom has it. He gets to you and to the players. They don't want to let him down. They realize how much he cares. When he asks something of them in terms of energy and effort, they don't want to let him down, so they play as hard as they can play, and they do it week after week."

So Allen arrived at Ben Davis High School on the west side of Indianapolis in 1998 to work under Dullaghan. Dominating success soon followed.

With Allen as the defensive coordinator, the Giants won Class 5A state championships in three of Dullaghan's last four seasons, including a pair of 15–0 years. Ben Davis was 76–10 during Allen's time there. Allen's passion was obvious.

"I remember a game," Dullaghan says, "where our defense intercepted a pass, and the kid ran it back for a touchdown. Tom darn near beat him to the goal line running down the sidelines. And when the kid came off the field, he jumps in Tom's arms, and his helmet hits Tom's head and cuts him. I remember Tom was bleeding.

"The enthusiasm and way he coached then, and still does, is pretty special."

During that time, Tracy taught in the night school program at Ben Davis and then went full time during the day. She taught algebra, geometry, calculus, and more.

"With all the moves we've made, I've taught every high school subject," she says with a laugh.

Dullaghan retired after the 2003 season and recommended Ben Davis hire Allen as head coach. The Giants did, and Allen went 25–12 in three seasons.

He seemed set for a long run of success, but he wanted a new challenge: college coaching. Making that kind of move came with risks. He'd take a hit in salary. He'd have to start at the bottom and work his way up. There was no guarantee of success. Tom was fine with it.

Was Tracy?

## CHAPTER 5

# Risky Business

A SINGLE GUY COULD DO SOMETHING LIKE THIS—A GUY with no family, no wife, no kids, maybe no house. He could take a chance on college coaching, and if it didn't work out, no harm. But these stakes were far higher. At Ben Davis, Allen had a great job with a good salary, health insurance, and other benefits. Beyond that, this was one of the best coaching situations in the state, regardless of sport. Ben Davis was a big school with plenty of resources. He could do great things there. Dick Dullaghan certainly had.

But a person dreams. What did Allen really want to do? What defined him?

There is the belief that a job isn't who you are but what you do, and for most that's true. But for those with a passion for what they do, a job is defining—it reflects character, belief, the ability to get the most out of yourself and those around you.

Reward comes with risk, and Allen had to ask himself, was the risk worth it?

Dullaghan provided an example. After successful high school runs at Bishop Chatard and Carmel, he had coached receivers for a couple of years at Purdue in the early 1980s and then spent a season as Army's offensive coordinator before taking over at Ben Davis. He knew the challenges that college coaching presented.

"Dick Dullaghan had influence," Tom Allen Sr. says. "Dick loved the college experience. He encouraged Tommy to try it.

"Dick would tell me when recruiters from Michigan, Notre Dame, Indiana, and Purdue would come to Ben Davis, he'd tell them, 'I've got a coach who can coach with you in the NFL or at any level he wants.' Dick saw something in him. That was probably Tommy's greatest influence."

Basically, Dullaghan encouraged Allen to follow his heart.

"He told me that, 'I want to go to college. I've reset my goals and would like to be a college coach and ultimately a defensive coordinator at the Big Ten level,'" Dullaghan says.

Allen was ready for one of the biggest decisions of his life.

"It was a big risk, but it was an easy decision," Allen says. "I knew in my heart what I wanted. I would have lived with a lot of regret if I had never taken the opportunity to try college football.

"Now I wasn't guaranteed the outcome and how long it would last. The risk involved the [high school] retirement [money]. You lose all that. You lose the guarantee of a lot of things. When you get into college, you're tied to the head coach. There are a lot of unknowns. You don't know the level you'll end up.

"I had many people who thought I was crazy, especially going to a non–head coaching position or a non-coordinator position. I was the special teams coordinator [at Wabash], but that's not the same as being the defensive coordinator. Many thought it wasn't a good move. They were like, 'What are you doing?'

"The ones who were in college said, 'If you want to coach college, you've got to go do it.' Wabash was a great opportunity with a program that had been successful with a great head coach [Chris Creighton]. From my perspective, yes, risky, but I was willing to take that risk.

"It's not the normal path. Most people haven't done it that way. It was definitely unorthodox."

Then Allen did what he does best—he got everybody to buy in. It started with Tracy, who would bear a heavy burden. Because of the workload, including recruiting, college coaches are rarely home. In some ways, she would almost be a single mom, taking care of the kids, the house, the yard, the transportation, the extracurricular activities, and everything else.

It was even more hectic for Tracy, who worked full time as a high school math teacher.

"The beauty of all this was I was very naïve," she says. "I never anticipated living in seven states in ten years. So I was all for it.

"I remember sitting in our living room when we were at Ben Davis. I specifically asked him what the dream was. He said, 'I want to be a Big Ten defensive coordinator.' I said, 'OK, let's go.' Over time, his dream has become our dream."

The dream began at Wabash College, a successful program in the small Indiana town of Crawfordsville, about an hour west of Indianapolis. Allen would coach special teams and the secondary in the fall of 2007 for head coach Chris Creighton.

"When we made the jump to Wabash," Tracy says, "Tom drove back and forth from Indianapolis the whole spring. He kept his job at Ben Davis. It was not your typical 'you come in January and we'll hire you.' Wabash didn't have the resources to do that."

That summer, the Allens sold their house and moved to Crawfordsville. Wabash had a big year, going 11–2 and reaching the NCAA Division III quarterfinals, and, by December, Creighton had left Wabash to take over the Drake program.

Allen scrambled to find another job.

"You win eleven games, and you're out of a job," Tracy says. "It was like, 'So this is college football.'"

Then it was on to Lambuth (defensive coordinator) in 2008, Drake (defensive coordinator) in 2010, Arkansas State (linebackers coach) in 2011, Mississippi (linebackers, special teams) in 2012, and South Florida (defensive coordinator) in 2015.

"Every place he went," Dullaghan says, "you could see his influence on the defense. You saw the enthusiasm and motivational skill he possesses. And he got tremendous experience."

Allen also got a tough lesson in college coaching reality. Every team he coached on had success, which meant the head coach got a better job, which meant Allen had to scramble to find another job.

He went to Lambuth in Tennessee under head coach Hugh Freeze. At that time, he and Tracy had three small children and lots of uncertainty. They rented a one-bedroom apartment and made the best of it.

"I bought the kids cots," Tracy says. "I slept on a loveseat every night.

"I'll never forget that first night. I put the cots down, and the kids were like, 'This is fun.' I'm crying. They thought it was a blast. I'm crying. It was hard. Tom's gone. I don't know who Hugh Freeze is. I don't know what Lambuth is. First time I saw the school, the facilities were worse than any high school we'd been at. I was like, 'What are we doing?'"

Still, in two years, Lambuth went 8–4 and 12–1. That earned Freeze the head coaching job at Arkansas State. It got Allen another job search.

"In our first three years in college, we lost less than five games," Tracy says, "and he was without a job again.

"There were high schools wanting him back. I was like, 'Is this what it's going to be like? We win, the head coach advances, and you're without a job all the time.'

"It was very frightening. We had young children. At that point, we had to decide do we keep fighting and pursuing the dream, or do we go back to high school?"

One of those high school possibilities, Tracy says, was Bloomington South High School.

Then Chris Creighton called with a job opportunity at Drake. Allen was there a year, and then Freeze called with a job offer at Arkansas State. A year after that, Freeze got the head coaching job at the SEC's Mississippi. This time, he took Allen with him.

The Allens spent three years at Mississippi. The Rebels went 24–15 and ranked among the SEC's best defenses. The year before Allen's arrival, Mississippi had been last in the SEC in total defense.

In 2015, Allen took the defensive coordinator job at South Florida. That was another risk. Head coach Willie Taggart had gone 2–10 and 4–8 in his first two seasons. Speculation had him on the hot seat. One more losing season and he might be fired. There was the chance this could be another one-and-done move for the Allens. Making it worse, South Florida opened 1–3, while Mississippi started 4–0 and ranked in the top twenty.

"At times you think, 'What have we done?'" Tracy says. "Tom never blinked. He said, 'God told me to take this job; we're going to be OK. If we get fired, we'll be OK. If we win, that's great.'"

South Florida won seven of its next eight games to earn a bid to the Miami Beach Bowl. Allen's defense led the American Athletic Conference by allowing just 19.6 points in conference play.

"It looked like it was a risky move," Tracy says, "but he thought it was the right move. He's pretty brave, focused, and determined. That's why I call him the Lion Chaser."

As it turned out, the chasing wasn't over. Neither was the risk. In January of 2016 came Hoosier opportunity. Indiana was a defensive mess that had lasted a generation. The Hoosiers scored big and allowed bigger. Head coach Kevin Wilson had fired his two previous defensive coordinators and was scouring the country looking for the right person for the job. The name Tom Allen kept popping up.

"In January of 2016, Kevin Wilson called me," Dullaghan says. "I was in Florida on vacation. He said, 'Dick, tell me why I should *not* hire Tom Allen.' I said, 'I promise you, if you hire him, there will be a culture change in your program. There was in mine when he came. He's had the same effect most every place he's been.'

"If you want a guy who will scream and cuss and berate players, rip their butts and attack them personally, that's not who you want. He is a teacher. He's a master motivator. He's a guy who knows how to get to a kid's hot button. He knows how to love them into submission, and they play unselfishly for the good of the team.

"I think Kevin had already decided he was going to hire Tom. I was pleased when he was hired. I've been in Indiana most of my life. Even though I coached at Purdue for three years, I was tickled to death to see Tom go to Indiana."

Allen's impact was dramatic in that 2016 season. Against a schedule that featured four top-ten opponents, the Hoosiers became a defensive force. They held teams to 380.1 total yards, an improvement of 129.4 yards from the previous season, and the best in the country. They allowed 10.4 fewer points and gave up 25 fewer touchdowns.

"It was obvious in 2016 that there was a culture change in defense," Dullaghan says. "It was there. It was obvious. Everybody in the whole country saw it."

That included IU athletic director Fred Glass, who was about to make his own dramatic change in the football program.

## CHAPTER 6

# Why Tom Allen?

FRED GLASS WAS ABOUT TO ROCK INDIANA'S FOOTBALL world with a 1–2 punch no one saw coming.

Kevin Wilson, fresh off a fourth straight victory over Purdue—something that hadn't happened . . . ever—and consecutive bowl berths, was out as head coach. The given reason—philosophical differences—was as mysterious as a quantum physics equation.

No matter. Wilson was gone, and Glass needed about five seconds to find his replacement—a man who had never been a college head coach.

Tom Allen.

"I still remember our first conversation, when Kevin Wilson was thinking of hiring Tom and asked me to talk to him," Glass says. "I was pacing around my dining room table, talking to him on the phone for around forty-five minutes and being incredibly impressed with his philosophy. He had some of my personal beliefs, such as kids have to believe you care about them before they'll perform at their highest level. They also have to believe you know what you're doing.

"Tom had both of those things in spades. I was very impressed with him from that first call. I became more so as things went along. Kevin hired him to be the head coach of the defense, and he did just that. I don't think that's a huge leap to become the head coach of the entire team."

From a national perspective, hiring Allen without even considering a national search made no sense. Every school conducts national searches these days, and not doing so sets you up for failure, criticism, and, perhaps, an exit out of town.

Glass didn't care. He had seen the improvement Allen had made with IU's perennially bad defense in just one year. That included holding teams to 10.4 points fewer than the previous season. Glass was convinced the right man for the job was already in the building. He wasn't about to lose him.

"It was very clear to me we had our guy in Tom Allen," he says. "I had no interest in a national search because I didn't want anybody else.

"I think every good athletic director, for all his coaches, has a list of the six best coaches in that sport. The first person on the list is always the person you have. Then you need to be ready. Somebody could get run over by a bus or get a better job or whatever. It was not like I was unaware of who potentially could be out there. I think I had a good grasp of who the top half dozen candidates would be if we ran a national search.

"I would prefer Tom Allen to all of those. That's not a criticism of the potential pool, but Tom is such a great fit. I think fit is so important. Not only the obvious piece that he's an Indiana guy, born [in the state], raised on football and basketball, Indianapolis football powerhouse Ben Davis head coach, and all that.

"I think he's the complete package for us and the kind of guy who can win here, which takes a certain type of person. I think Tom is that person."

Former IU football coach Bill Mallory, who took the Hoosiers to six bowls during his run in the 1980s and '90s, saw what Glass saw. He said there are similarities in the way they coach. He said they first met when Allen was a high school coach and came to one of his summer camps.

"As Tom progressed," Mallory said, "I got to know him better. I always had lot of great respect for him. He had a good reputation. When he came here, I knew he would be a good hire. I was pleased to see him get the head coaching job. He's a good, caring person. A good people person.

"He cares about the people around him, the players and coaches. He just has that approach. He's a darn good coach. His focus is more on the defense side, but he understands offense too. He's surrounded by a good staff.

"They're in good position to take this program and go on with it. They've been close, but that word, 'finish,' they have to get over the hump. I try to get out once or twice to watch practice [Tuesday and Thursday]. I like to watch the players and the way the coaches work with them. I'm impressed with the whole setup."

The opportunity caught Allen and his family by surprise.

"I don't know that we ever dreamed of being a head coach," Tracy Allen says. "Tom was getting older. When he wakes up in the morning, defense excites him. I don't know that he ever planned for being a head coach.

"Some other places had reached out to him for head coaching jobs. We started to think about it. He was very happy being a defensive coordinator. This was not a dream but an opportunity that God placed in front of him.

"Initially we had some strong mixed emotions. We felt bad for the Wilsons. If you dream about getting a head coaching job, you don't dream of getting it in these circumstances, of hurting someone else. I feel bad about that. Usually in this profession, the success of one is at the demise of someone else."

Allen couldn't overcome Indiana's struggling football tradition in his first season. The Hoosiers finished 5–7.

Mallory's advice: keep pushing. It took Mallory three years to build a winner.

"Tom is on track," Mallory said. "He knows what he's doing. His coaches know what they're doing.

"The big thing with Tom is he's very focused and positive. I go to practice. I see it. He's into it. Sure, he gets after players with tough love, firmness. What he's doing is right. I feel so confident in what they're doing here. I feel they'll continually get better.

"I told Tom, 'Keep doing what you're doing. It will pay dividends down the road.'"

Bob Hammel, the award-winning former sports columnist for the *Bloomington Herald-Times*, is just as optimistic.

"What's unusual about Tom is he's basically willing to turn that offense over to somebody else [offensive coordinator Mike DeBord]. A lot of defensive coaches who become head coaches want to do both offense and defense, but he seems comfortable not doing that. I think it will work."

Voice of the Hoosiers announcer Don Fischer sees a lot of former IU coach Bill Mallory in Allen.

"One thing I see that's the same in Tom as with Bill is the respect the players have for him. Even though he's a tough guy and he's demanding and puts the bar up here, you think, *How am I going to get up there?*

"That's what he demands of you. He does it in a way that doesn't make it negative. He sets the bar like a parent should. It's like, 'Hey, that's not good enough.'

"Make sure they understand that's what you expect from them because they're capable of more than that. That's what Bill did, and I see the same thing in Tom Allen. This guy thinks you can be better than you are. He'll try to help these kids buy into the fact that they can be better than what they think they can be.

"Somehow, someway, he gets through to those kids. It's very successful. He's done it every place he's been with the defenses. Think about it. In one year's time, they get dramatically better on defense. They go from the No. 120 or whatever defense to the fifties. How is that possible? It's the buy-in from the kids based on what this coach is telling them because we didn't get any better talent. Whatever he's selling, you'd better buy it."

Tracy Allen learned to buy in a long time ago without sacrificing her own career. She has her own successful educational consulting firm, Stop Chapter Testing.

"We went to the Big Ten meetings in Chicago, and to see Tom sitting next to all those Big Ten coaches, it was like, 'Wow, what have we got ourselves into?'

"For Tom, he loves Indiana. This is his home. His family is here. It's a dream opportunity for sure. It's maybe not the job that everybody would love, but he loves it. He loves his players. Indiana is filled with some great men. We're blessed to be part of something so special."

## CHAPTER 7

# Coaching to His Strengths

IT STARTS WITH PLAYERS. IT HAS TO. IF YOU DON'T HAVE good players, caring players, players who understand it's team over individual, you have no chance.

So what is a Tom Allen player?

"A tough, hard-nosed kid who loves to compete," he says. "That's what I want. To me, mixed in with that, a guy who cares about school. A guy I learn to trust. Those are the guys I want to surround myself with."

Allen wants to win now and for years to come. Having sustained success, he says, starts with "recruiting to your culture. Get guys who fit what you want. The ability to recruit to that. It's about getting those right guys. When you have the right guys who believe and have bought in to what you're doing, then you can make that happen. I believe you get that when you recruit the family for a whole year; then you have that success. That's how it perpetuates itself."

It also means blending intensity with fun, a trait Allen has always had. His son, Thomas, saw that while his father was coaching at Ben Davis.

"Every place he's been, he's high intensity," Thomas says. "At Ben Davis, one time he came home with a black eye because he got into a dogpile after a pick-6. That's the kind of guy he is. It doesn't matter how old he gets, he's the same way, with a lot of intensity. That's what makes him special."

Behind the scenes, Allen doesn't intimidate or make life miserable for those around him. Little things matter in the way he treats people as well as the way he coaches. When he became head coach, he made it a point to get to know everyone in the program, including interns. He wanted to make sure they knew they were appreciated.

Case in point—senior staff assistant Kate Miller, invaluable for her behind-the-scenes ability to do what needs to be done, was organizing a staff trip to Indianapolis for some meetings. She ordered everyone dinner from Panera. That included Allen. Afterward she found out Allen didn't like Panera.

"It was his least favorite place to eat, but he didn't say anything. He said, 'You'd already taken orders. I didn't want to be the difficult coach.' I said, 'But you're the head coach. You're allowed to be the difficult one.'

"But that's not him. What stands out to me is how polite he is. He's very calm when he's in the office—nothing is flying off the handle or gets extreme. In practice, the intensity really ramps up."

Some head coaches become prima donnas, expecting others to do things for them as if their staff were servants. Not Allen.

"He's very down-to-earth," Miller says. "His wife helps keep him grounded. She doesn't want anyone driving him around. Sometimes when you're a head coach, you kind of have to. They get so busy that they need help so they can work while driving. His wife says, 'You can drive yourself.'"

Beyond that, Miller says, "It's little things. Like carrying luggage off a plane on a trip. He carries as much as the support staff and managers do. If we can do it, he can do it. You don't see that often in Power 5 conference, big-time football."

If quirks intrigue you, consider that Allen is a big Mountain Dew fan. It helps him stay awake during all the late-night sessions, and if you're a coach, you have plenty of those. Allen had plenty of late sessions while preparing for Utah in the 2016 Foster Farms Bowl in California. Video coordinator Joel Baron was there to help via a nearby convenience store.

"I bought all the twenty-ounce Mountain Dews the store had so he could keep working on the game plan," Baron says with a smile.

Former IU safeties coach Noah Joseph (now at Rutgers) saw Allen in action every day, first as the defensive coordinator, then as the head coach.

"His first priority is to connect to you as a person," Joseph says. "He wants to connect with you—player, coach, support staff, trainer—it doesn't matter. He'll connect to you as a person. You feel you have a relationship. He trusts you, and you trust him. If there's an issue, you can go to him, or he can go to you. You can get something accomplished. That's the number-one thing.

"He's a fantastic motivator. Whether it's through something he's read, a movie he's watched, a song he's listened to. . . . He can transform a thought into how it affects our team and how he can . . . tie it together.

"Then he's smart. He understands how teams will try to attack his defense and what he's trying to do. 'If they do this, I can make this subtle adjustment, so if they think we're going to do this, we'll do that.'

"Those things make him who he is. They make him a special person."

After engineering one of the nation's biggest defensive turnarounds in 2016 in his first season as IU's defensive coordinator, Tom Allen was named the program's twenty-ninth head coach on December 1, 2016.

As the Hoosiers head coach, Allen has continued many of the program's long-standing traditions, including the touching of Hep's Rock before the start of each home game. Located behind Memorial Stadium's north end zone, Hep's Rock is in memory of former Indiana coach Terry Hoeppner, who passed away in 2007.

After dismissing Coach Kevin Wilson late in the 2016 season, Indiana University athletic director Fred Glass (right) wasted little time in finding a new permanent replacement. Glass bypassed conducting a national coaching search and instead opted to quickly promote Allen to head coach before the 2016 Foster Farms Bowl.

During his prep coaching days, Tom Allen got invaluable insight from his father, Tom Allen Sr., at Ben Davis High School. During the current IU head coach's three seasons as the Giants' head coach from 2004–06, the program went 25–12.

At Ben Davis, Allen was a part of three state championship teams as an assistant coach. The Giants won in 1999, 2001, and 2002. Ben Davis went 76–10 in Allen's six years under legendary coach Dick Dullaghan.

Ken Kaczmarek was an All-Big Ten linebacker in 1967 after
leading the Hoosiers with 118 tackles. His biggest play came in the
regular-season finale against Purdue, when his forced fumble in
the closing minutes helped secure IU's 19–14 win. Kaczmarek was
inducted into the Indiana University Athletics Hall of Fame in 2017.

The 2017 season marked the fiftieth anniversary of the Hoosiers' 1967 Big Ten championship season and the trip to the 1968 Rose Bowl. The Hoosiers have earned only ten bowl trips since that championship season, with the lone wins coming at the 1979 Holiday Bowl, 1988 Peach Bowl, and 1991 Copper Bowl.

*Left*, Lee Corso compiled a 41–68–2 record in ten seasons as the Hoosiers' coach from 1973–82, highlighted by the 1979 season, when IU went 8–4 and defeated BYU 38–37 in the Holiday Bowl. Corso remains one of only two IU coaches to ever win a bowl game. The other is Bill Mallory.

*Above,* After a thirty-five-year absence from Bloomington, Lee Corso returned for the Hoosiers' 2017 season-opener against Ohio State with ESPN's *College GameDay* crew. Corso was presented with the Bill Orwig Award for outstanding contributions made by a non-alumnus at the end of the first quarter of the game and was subsequently carried off the field by many of his former players who were in attendance.

*Facing,* After being fired by IU following the 1982 season, Lee Corso coached for one year at Northern Illinois (1984) and one more with the USFL's Orlando Renegades (1985). After the conclusion of his coaching career, he joined ESPN with the 1993 debut of *College GameDay*, a role he's held ever since.

Anthony Thompson is the most decorated player in Indiana football history. In addition to finishing as the runner-up for the 1989 Heisman Trophy, Thompson was a two-time Big Ten MVP who once held the NCAA career record for touchdowns (65). He was inducted into the College Football Hall of Fame in 2007.

Anthony Thompson rushed for 1,793 yards and 24 touchdowns as a senior in 1989. In addition to finishing second to Houston's Andre Ware for the Heisman Trophy, Thompson was tabbed as college football's player of the year by the Walter Camp Foundation and was the recipient of the Maxwell Award as the year's top player.

*Above*, While it had been more than twenty years since Bill Mallory (left) last coached a football game at IU, he remained a welcomed presence at practices and games until his death in 2018. He also had two sons coach at IU—Doug (1994–96) and Curt (2002–04).

*Above,* In Allen's one season as Indiana's defensive coordinator, his impact was significant. IU yielded 380.1 yards/game in 2016 compared to 509.5 yards/game in 2015. For his efforts, Allen was a nominee for the 2016 Broyles Award as college football's assistant coach of the year.

*Facing,* Tom Allen and his wife, Tracy, met as freshmen in college and were married soon after graduation in 1992. In the subsequent years, the pair has moved eleven times for different coaching jobs at both the high school and collegiate levels, culminating in the decision to leave South Florida in 2016 to join the IU staff.

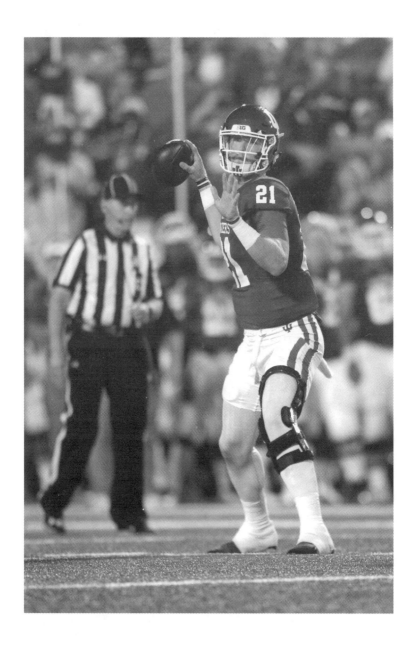

*Above,* Wide receiver Simmie Cobbs was clearly the Hoosiers' difference-maker on offense in 2017, ranking second in the Big Ten in receptions (72) and fourth in receiving yards (841). After earning first-team All-Big Ten honors, Cobbs announced his intentions to bypass his senior season and made himself eligible for the NFL draft.

*Facing,* After an honorable mention All-Big Ten season as a junior, quarterback Richard Lagow entered the 2017 season as the team's starter. Lagow's early-season struggles, though, prompted a move to true freshman Peyton Ramsey by the third game. Lagow eventually regained the starting role after Ramsey suffered a knee injury, and Lagow ultimately threw for 1,936 yards and 15 touchdowns.

*Above,* Cornerback Rashard Fant (16) was another big reason behind Indiana's defensive turnaround in recent years. Fant earned All-Big Ten recognition in 2016 and 2017, and finished his IU career as the program's all-time leader in passes defensed and passes broken up.

*Facing,* Few Hoosier football players made as big an impact as linebacker Tegray Scales. The Cincinnati, Ohio, product became IU's first All-America linebacker since 1987 when he earned the honor in 2016 after totaling a Big Ten-best 126 tackles along with a nation's best 23.5 tackles for loss.

*Above,* While Indiana entered the 2017 season expecting to be led by a fifth-year senior quarterback, Allen quickly turned to a true freshman—Peyton Ramsey—to lead the offense. Ramsey threw for 1,252 yards and 10 touchdowns before having his season cut short by a knee injury.

*Facing top,* Current Indiana offensive coordinator Mike DeBord first met Tom Allen when DeBord was an assistant coach at Michigan. DeBord recruited the state of Indiana for the Wolverines. That brought him to Ben Davis High School when Allen was an assistant coach there.

*Facing bottom,* Indiana defensive line coach Mark Hagen joined the Hoosiers' staff about one month after Allen arrived in 2016. Hagen, who has more than twenty years of coaching experience in the Big Ten and SEC, was a standout linebacker at Indiana from 1988–91, leading Bill Mallory's teams in tackles from 1989–91.

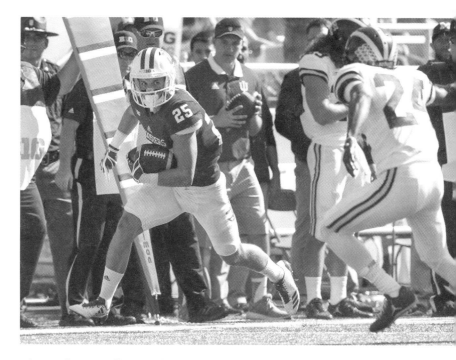

*Above,* A former walk-on, Luke Timian ranked third in the Big Ten and thirty-ninth nationally with 68 receptions in 2017. His reception total ranks seventh on IU's all-time single-season list, behind some of the program's all-time greats such as James Hardy and Cody Latimer.

*Facing top,* After consistently rating as one of the Big Ten's worst defenses, linebacker Chris Covington (4) and the rest of the Indiana unit have been one of the nation's most improved in the last two years. In 2017, Indiana ranked sixth in the Big Ten in total defense and fourth in pass defense.

*Facing bottom,* While Indiana's 2017 squad had plenty of veterans, several newcomers made significant contributions as well. Freshman wide receiver Whop Philyor (22) earned Big Ten Network All-Freshman honors after catching 33 passes for 335 yards and 3 touchdowns. Included in that total was a 13-catch, 127-yard performance at Maryland that put Philyor fourth on IU's all-time single-game receptions list.

*Above,* As Tom Allen looks to build a consistent winner at Indiana, he's well aware of the struggles that many coaches before him have had. It's been more than seventy years since Indiana had a football coach who finished with a winning record (Bo McMillin, 63–48–11 from 1934 to '47).

*Facing top,* Chase Dutra concluded his IU career with 237 tackles in 42 games. Dutra saved his best for last, leading the Hoosiers with 96 tackles, including 65 solo stops, in 2017. The Brownsburg, Indiana, native was also IU's Special Teams Player of the Year.

*Facing bottom,* Jonathan Crawford turned in one of his best games in the Hoosiers' loss at Penn State, recording an interception and a blocked field goal. Crawford has been an anchor of Indiana's defense since arriving from Largo, Florida, starting all 38 games in his first three seasons.

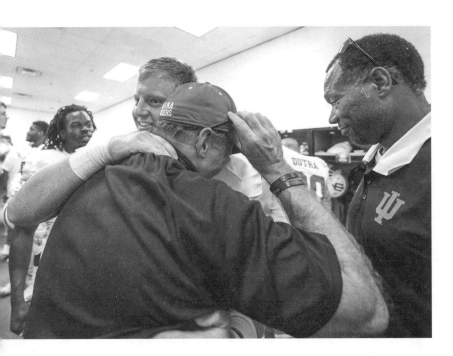

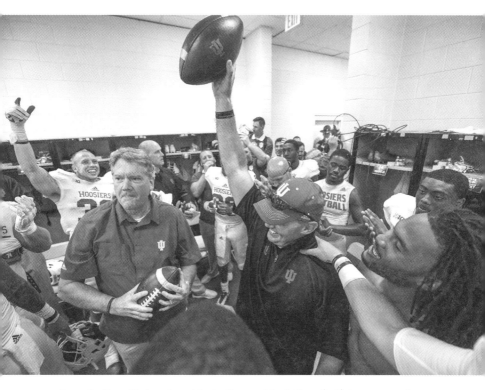

*Above,* Indiana University athletic director Fred Glass (left) is convinced Tom Allen will bring a consistent winning football program to Bloomington.

*Facing top,* One of the highlights of the 2017 season was a convincing 34–17 victory at Virginia, a team that would go on to become bowl eligible later in the season. The win was the first for Tom Allen as a Division I head coach.

*Facing bottom,* While Allen's debut 5–7 season wasn't the record that IU had hoped for, there were plenty of signs of progress. Five of Indiana's seven losses came against ranked teams, including three against top-five foes. Indiana was either tied or leading in the second halves in three of those five games.

## CHAPTER 8

# Love Will Find a Way

ALLEN ARRIVED AS DEFENSIVE COORDINATOR IN 2016 with relationship building as a top priority. Do that and you have trust, loyalty, and the intangible feeling that everyone has each other's back, a collective will to not let an individual fail because of the team consequence.

"In my first meeting with our defense, I wrote the letters L-E-O on the board," Allen says. "I asked them if they knew what that meant. They didn't. It stands for 'Love Each Other.' Didn't talk about football. Didn't talk about schemes. It was about changing the mind-set and the culture of that side of the football.

"To me, it was about getting our focus off ourselves, building trust, developing a culture that says it's not about 'me'; it's about 'we.' 'I don't truly care who gets the credit. I care that this team is successful.' That's the attitude that I wanted. That's what I wanted in our team.

"L-E-O is a big deal for us. And I tell our coaches that it starts with us, and that helps it filter throughout the program."

That didn't change when Allen became head coach.

"It's L-E-O," he says. "It's all centered on the fact that it's not all about me. It's centered on the fact that I'm going to do things that allow the guys around me to have success. When we do well together, the individuals get recognized. I want that mind-set. It's not normal. It's not what is often maybe advertised, but I believe that's the key."

So Allen mentions L-E-O at the end of press conferences, during team meetings, individual meetings, and, perhaps, even while checking out at grocery stores. The man is obsessed, and in this change-the-culture environment, that's a very good thing.

"Having an environment where when you truly care about the people around you, you understand that my decisions affect everybody else," Allen says. "The highest level of accountability is to make decisions that affect you, understand it affects you, and I'm also man enough to stand up and hold you accountable as a teammate. That's what I want.

"That's hard to do with your peers. It's hard to be able to say to one of your friends, 'You shouldn't do this.' It's hard to get on a guy for whatever, even on the practice field, when we're running, while we're conditioning, when you're off socially, whatever. But that's what I want.

"To me, that's a powerful thing that doesn't just happen. Everybody talks about family. Every program in America talks about that. A lot of times it's just that; it's talk. I want it lived out. I want it to be felt.

"When you're playing for the people around you, that's when it's special. It's very shallow when it's just about you.

"That's the culture I want. We're going to just keep creating it, keep working at it. And when you get it, you've got to work hard to keep it. We're not where we want to be yet, but that's what we want to continue to work on."

Saying it is one thing. Coaching to it is another. How does Allen do that? What signs are there that he, like Bill Mallory a generation earlier, is the right man for this cream 'n' crimson job?

That answer comes by hitting the road.

## CHAPTER 9

# Illinois Immersion

TOM ALLEN BENT A KNEE.

Before the game that would determine, for one week at least, if Hoosier bowl hopes would survive, before a postgame celebration that would include players giving him a game ball for his first Big Ten victory, Allen moved away from everyone to a corner of the small visiting locker room at Illinois's Memorial Stadium to pray and reflect.

Faith mattered. Belief mattered. Beyond strategy and effort and resilience, it came down to being a part of something bigger than yourself. It's how Allen connects to players and people, how he determines what has true meaning for them. He doesn't push or preach religion, but he also is true to himself. In a few minutes, Allen would talk to the players one last time before hitting the field amid win-or-else pressure. But first, before competitive battle, he took time for faith.

The Hoosiers (3–6) had to sweep their final three games—Illinois, Rutgers, and Purdue—to become bowl eligible for the third straight season. If they couldn't beat the Illini, which, like IU, was 0–6 in the Big Ten, their postseason hopes were over.

Keys were simple: generate more takeaways (IU only had 7, the fewest in the Big Ten; Illinois had a conference-worst 19 turnovers); kick-start the Big Ten's worst rushing attack (the Hoosiers averaged just 114.5 yards a game) against the league's worst run defense (Illinois allowed 205.7 yards); and exploit the Illini's man coverage preference by getting the ball to superstar receiver Simmie Cobbs (he had 15 catches for 200 yards and 3 touchdowns in his previous two games).

Oh, and win.

The Big Ten road can be a brutal place to do that, even against a team as young and beat-up as Illinois.

Here's what it's like to make a trip and find previously elusive success.

⊸⊰⊱⊷

A winter-like cold swept into Bloomington the Friday before the game, but at least it was clear and sunny, unlike, say, Northwestern, where snow pounded Evanston.

Players began with 8:00 a.m. treatment, then breakfast. There was a ten-minute team meeting, a thirty-minute special teams meeting, and half-hour meetings with the offense and defense. Then there was a seventy-minute practice followed by another treatment session and then lunch.

Five buses gathered in a Memorial Stadium parking lot. There were two buses for offensive players and coaches; two for defensive players, specialists, and coaches; and one for staff and guests.

Getting to Illinois was more complicated because of the seemingly never-ending I-69 construction north of Bloomington. The plan was to take Highway 46 west to Spencer then go north on Highway 231 to Crawfordsville before getting on I-74 for the final leg to Champaign, Illinois. A police escort ensured the buses could cruise through intersections, stop signs, and stoplights.

After a three-hour drive, the team arrived at Hawthorne Suites, which was a ten-minute walk from the Illinois version of Memorial Stadium.

There was no settling-in time. Players got off the bus and gathered in a hotel hallway, where drinks and light food were available. If you went hungry or thirsty, it was your own fault and would put you in strength coach Keith Caton's doghouse.

"Make sure you hydrate," Caton said in a voice that could bend steel.

The original plan was to give players twenty-five minutes to settle into their rooms before doing a stretch/walk-through session. That was scrapped. Players quickly went outside to the back parking lot for the walk-through.

The sun was setting. Pink and gold colored the sky. And it was cold. A brisk wind provided an uncomfortable edge.

No matter.

Players divided into offensive and defensive groups and went through a half-hour walk-through session. A police officer provided security.

At that point it became clear—senior Richard Lagow would start at quarterback. An injured Peyton Ramsey, who had become the starter a month earlier, couldn't go, although that hadn't been announced. He hadn't practiced all week. You could get away with that if you were, say, offensive lineman Coy Cronk, who had barely practiced in recent weeks because of his own injury (Allen called him a warrior who refused to not play), but the quarterback position was too complex to play without practice, especially for a young quarterback. So Lagow, who had started the first four games and who had come off the bench in recent weeks because of Ramsey's knee injury, would run the offense.

After the walk-through, the players gathered in a ballroom for a special teams meeting. A large video screen flashed images. No, it wasn't the trailer for the newest *Star Wars* movie.

"We're locked in!" Allen shouted. He wanted players mentally engaged. The stakes were too high for them not to be. "Focus. Focus. Focus."

The first video involved kicking extra points and field goals. Offensive line coach Darren Hiller ran it. A series of short clips provided Hoosier keys on what to look for and what to do.

"Jacob," he said to defensive tackle Jacob Robinson, "do you see this on the edge?"

"Yes, sir."

Later, Hiller addressed a couple of other players on what to look for.

"You guys good?"

"Yes, sir," they said in unison.

Then it switched to punts. Safeties coach Noah Joseph took over.

"Shock and snatch, and then free to the ball," he said.

Then came kickoff coverage with linebackers coach William Inge.

"When you have a chance to make a play, make it," Inge said. "Make it happen."

Later, he addressed linebacker Kiante Walton. "What you got here, Kiante? Turn it back in."

"Yes, sir."

Next up was cornerbacks coach Brandon Shelby with a look at punt returns. He made multiple points, each time ending with, "Do you understand?"

"Yes, sir," the players said.

"Get it done."

"Legal blocks, Jonah," Shelby told receiver Jonah Morris. "Be a ball player."

"Yes, sir."

Running backs coach Mike Hart had kickoff returns. He listed the top four goals: secure the ball, get off the blocks, no penalties, and score.

"If we've got a crease, we've got to stay on our feet, right, Devonte?" Hart said.

"Yes, sir," tailback Devonte Williams said.

Then it switched to offensive and defensive meetings. Offensive coordinator Mike DeBord took charge of the offense, showing video of plays and scenarios the Hoosiers were likely to face. DeBord overcame a couple of video technical glitches to make his point: protect the ball. He showed a defensive clip from a previous Illinois game. The opponent's running back was about to fumble.

"This running back shows no pride in protecting the ball," DeBord said. "See how he has his elbows up? He doesn't secure the ball. Illinois's defense is taught to strip the ball."

Hiller, quarterbacks coach Nick Sheridan, and receivers coach Grant Heard also made points. Hiller said, "We've got to be alert for a blitz."

On Saturday morning, game day, there was another outside walk-through in the hotel parking lot and then more meetings. The team arrived at Memorial Stadium to loud rap music that reminded no one of, say, Barbra Streisand. It came from a small, rolling boom box pushed by a staff member. Not every player listened. Some had their own music via headsets.

The locker room rocked as players dressed. As they got ready to take the field, the music stopped. Some players talked quietly to each other. Some listened to their own music. Others just stared hard into space.

Inge strode among the players. "It's the calm before the storm. The calm before the storm. Bring your own juice. Get ready to whip tail!"

Most position coaches gathered their players for final instructions. Hiller offered a passionate message.

"Play outside your comfort zone. Do you understand? We've got to dominate the man in front of you. We will run the [bleeping] ball. Do you understand? We have to win the game upfront. Does everybody understand? Let's get it done."

Allen, a deeply religious man, took that knee for private prayer away from everybody. Then he addressed the Hoosiers. The locker room was small, so not every player could see him. "If you can't see, make sure your ears are open," he shouted. "I've been saying all week about a sense of urgency. Time creates that—in life and in football. That's a fact. When that becomes real to you, it changes how you do what you do. How hard you play. It changes things for the better. You embrace it. You embrace that mind-set.

"I chose that word for a reason. For *a reason*! For such a time as this."

His voice rose and grew hoarse.

"Focus on the very next play in front of you. That's the now. That's being in the moment. "I want to play *our* football. That's physical football! That's tough football! It's relentless football for sixty minutes and beyond. Whatever it takes. I want an edge all game long from this team. An edge. That's a clenched fist and a set jaw ready to smack somebody in the mouth for sixty minutes. That's who we are. That's when we're at our very best. That's what the seniors deserve. Do you understand me?"

"Yes, sir!" the Hoosiers said.

Allen told everyone to gather for a final word.

"Now on three," he said. "One, two, three—now!"

And then the Hoosiers charged onto the field, aiming to start a potential bowl-making run.

❖⟹ ⟸❖

For twenty-five minutes, IU controlled the game but not the score. The Hoosiers led 14–0 at halftime thanks to tailback Morgan Ellison's 3-yard touchdown run and tight end Ian Thomas's 4-yard TD catch from Lagow. Then they gave up a 77-yard touchdown pass on the first play of the third quarter, added Griffin Oakes's 28-yard field goal, and gave up another touchdown pass for a 17–14 lead before putting the Illini away with Lagow's 5-yard touchdown pass to Simmie Cobbs.

Final score: 24–14.

IU's defensive line attacked from the start to register 8 sacks—third most in school history—and ten tackles for loss. The defense also got two interceptions and a fumble recovery.

Lagow had been rattled, but not broken, by his earlier benching. Since returning to action, he'd completed 62 percent of his passes for 646 yards, 6 touchdowns, and 3 interceptions. He'd reduced the mistakes that contributed to him losing the starting job.

Against Illinois, he was 32 for 48 for 289 yards and 2 touchdowns.

"When the situation happened with the change," Cobbs said, "Richard kept his head high. He still stayed a leader. He still did everything he normally does in practice. You always want to emphasize the next man up. When Peyton went out, Richard stepped up like we expected him to. His confidence stayed the same."

Also stepping up was Rashard Fant, a fifth-year senior cornerback with a third straight bowl appearance very much on his mind. He had an interception and key pass coverage to seal the victory.

That made up for his couple of dropped interceptions and might have been sparked, Allen said, by his suggestion.

"I made him change gloves," Allen said. "He dropped two picks, fumbled a punt. I told him, 'Take those gloves off, put new ones on.' He got himself a pick, so it must have worked."

Added Fant, "I changed them and went to an older pair. It had nothing to do with the gloves. I've got to make the play."

He made a big one with an interception in the closing minutes to help preserve the victory.

"It's huge," Fant said. "It's all about finishing. We took a stride in being one of the best defenses in the Big Ten.

"I'm glad we were able to finish. We know we can do it. Now we can look for Rutgers and try and get another win."

The victory snapped a four-game IU losing streak and extended the Illini's losing streak to eight games.

It also gave Allen his first Big Ten win.

"It feels great," Allen said. "When you looked at the schedule, you knew it would be tough. You have to keep battling. All those games we were right there within one play. The first of anything is always special. It's one I'll always remember."

Added Cobbs, "We've been pushing all year, trying to finish the game. To get it done for him is an incredible feeling."

Allen had wanted the Hoosiers to play tough, physical, and relentless.

Under win-or-else pressure, they did.

IU rushed for 139 yards, with Cole Gest leading with 82.

"This gives us a lot of confidence," Cobbs said. "Glad we got the W. We'll prepare for Rutgers."

In a rocking postgame celebration, Allen was brief: "Road wins are tough. Get as loud as you want!"

Linebacker Tegray Scales presented Allen with the game ball. "Today Coach Allen got his first Big Ten win," he said, and the team erupted into clapping, yelling, and laughing.

"Keep fighting, baby!" Allen said. "Keep fighting for each other. Here we go!"

They sang the Indiana fight song three times—once loudly, once softly with plenty of finger snapping, then loudly again.

It harkened back to IU glory past, to a time when victories—and bowl appearances—were common. It was similar to another tough-minded Hoosier coach who resurrected the program to its best-ever run—more wins and more bowls than ever before.

CHAPTER 10

# The Mallory Years

BILL MALLORY JABS AN INDEX FINGER INTO THE AIR THE
way a gladiator would a spear.

"It should have been seven bowls!"

He spits out the words like verbal bullets. His eyes narrow. His
voice hardens. Physically he sits in the Memorial Stadium press box
in the fall of 2017. Emotionally he is back in 1994, near the end of the
most remarkable football run Indiana has ever seen.

Mallory took Indiana to six bowls in eight years, but in his mind,
it was seven bowls. In 1994, IU finished 6–5. It received an invitation
to the Motor City Bowl. Mallory wanted to go. Players and assistant
coaches wanted to go. But citing costs, Indiana administrators shot
it down. There would be no bowl.

"That still irks me," Mallory says.

Before Mallory arrived, IU had been to just two bowls in a history that began in 1887. It lost in the Rose Bowl to USC in January
of 1968 and beat Brigham Young in the Holiday Bowl in December
of 1979.

Mallory coached the Hoosiers to a football pinnacle. It was not
to the height of, say, Ohio State, but it reached a level never achieved
before or since.

He preferred substance over style, toughness over flash. He
coached hard-nosed, fundamentally sound teams, which meant
tough coaching that wouldn't always meet today's politically correct
standards. If you had to grab a guy's face mask or get a little physical

to make a point, you did it. If you had to speak the hard truth, and coach even harder, you did that as well.

It produced bowl victories, accolades, and more.

"I expected that hundred percent commitment," Mallory says. "It wasn't a sometimes thing. It was an all-times thing."

Mallory was famous for clichés (jaw locking and helmet strapping were among them) and for the impact they made based on his passion.

"He was not what you would call eloquent," former award-winning *Bloomington Herald-Times* sports editor/columnist Bob Hammel says, "but nobody moved a crowd better than he did."

Hammel offers an example from 1988.

"They'd lost to Kentucky the year before when somebody whiffed on a block during a fourth-and-goal run and AT [Anthony Thompson] got tackled.

"Bill was really fired up that next season. Kentucky was the home opener. He was at an IU fan event in Bloomington the week of the game. Here are these businessmen in suits, and they were ready to hit people, he had them so ready to play Kentucky. You can imagine what his players were like. He said, 'We're going to lock the gates and kick their ass!' It had such an effect. I quoted him. He was not pleased. He was so into it."

No Hoosier coach can match Mallory's six bowls. IU has made just three other bowls in its history. Beyond that, no IU coach ever started amid so much disarray. Mallory was the program's third coach in less than two years. Lee Corso was fired in 1982. Sam Wyche was hired and then left for the NFL's Cincinnati Bengals ten months later.

"Bill came on after an unstable period," Hammel said. "For those players in that first year, he was their third head coach in three years. I'm sure some heads were swimming. It was three totally different philosophies."

Recruiting was a mess. Apathy was rampant.

And then Mallory went to work.

"Not to make excuses," he says, "but they hadn't done any recruiting in the last few years. Sam Wyche had left within ten months right after the season to coach the Bengals. Lee Corso was terminated, so he didn't do any recruiting.

"They'd done nothing for two years. It was going to be thin city for a while. I knew that."

Mallory also knew how to fix it. It started with a strong staff of assistant coaches, men such as Buck Suhr, George Belu, Steve Stripling, Jim Muehling, Joe Novak, and Floyd Keith. They had coached with Mallory for years, developing a chemistry that helped build a winner.

"The staff he had was the best overall coaching staff we ever had here," award-winning radio announcer Don Fischer says. "They proved it over time. Those guys all coached really well, and they had to coach well because our teams got better quickly. Indiana went from 0–11 to 4–7 to a bowl game in the third year. Then it continued.

"The staff is what made the difference."

Darn right, Mallory says, in so many words.

"I had a great group of coaches. We'd all been together for a while. That was important."

Mallory's IU run ended after the 1996 season with 69 victories, the most by any coach in program history.

"Bill was the one guy in my experience who actually put a floor under Indiana," Hammel says. "You could count on a .500 season. Back in Indiana's history, which is pathetic, it's in the .300s rather than anything close to .500."

How did Mallory do it? Do his methods serve as a blueprint for Tom Allen to duplicate?

⋯⋙◉ ◉⋘⋯

Understanding why Bill Mallory thrived at Indiana means understanding Shawn Harper. Yes, Mallory coached plenty of outstanding players at IU, highlighted by Heisman Trophy runner-up Anthony Thompson. But the heart of what made Mallory a great coach, and an even better person, is personified by Harper, who was so far under the recruiting radar in high school that he didn't stir up a blip.

Harper came from a rough background in Columbus, Ohio. He'd grown up amid inner-city gangs, bounced around from foster home to foster home, and showed little academic discipline, ranking last in his high school graduating class of 157. But the Independence High School football coach saw promise and got Harper to come out for the team as a senior. He saw more promise and called Mallory, who had extensive contacts in Ohio from his playing and coaching days at Miami of Ohio and more.

"He said, 'I've got this young man who came out of nothing,'" Mallory says. "'Academically, he's right at the bottom of his class. He's not a dummy but just no focus. I put him in a junior college [North Iowa Area Community College]. Do me a favor. Check him out. I think he could be a good one for you.'"

Mallory checked. He brought the six-foot-three, 316-pound Harper in for a recruiting visit.

"I liked him. The coaches did too. I said, 'I'm going to make Shawn an offer. Give him an opportunity. He's a young man who deserves that.'"

Then Mallory went into coaching-force-of-nature mode.

"I sat him down and told him, 'I'll put you on scholarship.' Then I said, 'I'm going to tell you something. First of all, you're going to keep your rump clean. You won't do anything to give this program or university a bad name. Understand that?' He said yes.

"I said, 'Number two, you're going to go to class, and your rump is going to sit in the front row, and I'm going to check on you with my [graduate assistants], and you'd better be there, or I'll have you up in the morning at six o'clock, and you and I are going to work out and run. It will give me a chance to get my workout done in the morning. I'll get your rump up.' He said, 'Coach, you can count on me.'

"So I got a GA. I said, 'You're assigned to Harper. You check every class and let me know what you find. If he isn't there, that turkey is getting up in the morning.' The GA checked him and said, 'Shawn is in class, sitting in the front row. He smiled and gave me a little wave.' That went on for at least two weeks. He was committed."

As a junior college graduate, Harper had two years of eligibility at IU. He wasn't ready to contribute his first season, so Mallory redshirted him. The next year, Harper was ready and became a starter after the fourth game. As a senior, "he was one of the top offensive linemen in the Big Ten," Mallory says, and he earned All-Big Ten honors.

Mallory was interested in more than Harper's football talent. So was Buzz Kurpius, also known as Coach Buzz, IU's associate athletic director for academics, who became a mentor, tutor, and mother figure for countless Hoosier athletes over the years.

"Shawn was a severe stutterer," Mallory says. "I talked to Buzz and said, 'We have to help him. He's really struggling with his speech.' She got a speech therapist. The lady did a wonderful job. She was with him during his entire time at IU."

Harper wasn't drafted by an NFL team but did play eight games over several seasons for a couple of teams, including the Indianapolis Colts, before spending time in NFL Europe.

Finally, he realized it was time to move beyond football. Harper visited Mallory and told him he wanted to get into the security business. Mallory's brother Tom was an orthopedic surgeon whose building had a security service.

"Tom said, 'I'll go to bat for him,'" Mallory said.

The company hired him. Three years later, Harper started his own security business, American Service Protection.

But Harper had another goal—he wanted to be a motivational speaker. He talked to Mallory again.

"He said, 'I want to talk to those who are having difficulties. I want to talk to juniors and seniors in high school and go to juvenile delinquent centers on the side.'"

Harper did that as well. He's become a renowned motivational speaker.

"Two years ago, I'm in Naples, Florida," Mallory says. "Shawn calls me. He said, 'I'm speaking to high schools in Naples. Would you come?' I did. He was impressive. At Indiana, he was a young man who everyone took an interest in—Buzz and her staff, my coaches, professors. I can't say enough about how Shawn took advantage of that."

⋯⇒◉⇐⋯

Understanding why Mallory thrived at Indiana means understanding his competitiveness and toughness. In the early 1960s, he was a young assistant coach at Bowling Green. In 1964, the Falcons played Miami of Ohio, coached by Bo Schembechler, who gained lasting fame by later coaching at Michigan for the Mid-American Conference championship.

Mallory's youngest brother, Dave, was a Miami linebacker.

"He was a good linebacker," Mallory says. "I mean, he'd hit you. He was Bo's captain."

During the game, things got feisty.

"We're on the sidelines," Mallory says, "and Dave hits our running back when [the running back] was out of bounds. He knocks him clear into our bench. The official just stands there looking at him. I get in the official's ear and say, 'That guy hit him out of bounds; flag him!' Dave comes over and said to me, 'You eat [crap]!' An assistant coach next to me said, 'I thought your brother loved you?'"

Mallory laughs at the memory.

"I said, 'That's what you call brotherly love.'"

Before the game, Mallory gave the pregame talk right before the players hit the field. It didn't go as planned, says Bob Hammel.

"Bill got so into his pregame pep talk that he hyperventilated and collapsed," Hammel says with a laugh. "The players almost ran over him on their way to the field, and he's still out. The other coaches looked at him. Somebody said, 'I think he's dead.' [Head coach Doyt Perry] said, 'It's five minutes till kickoff, we gotta get out there.' The problem was, Bill was the defensive coordinator. He calls all the signals, and they got nobody to make the calls. So they revive him and get him out there."

For the record, Bowling Green won.

"Bo used the Mallorys as the definition of competitiveness," Hammel says. "He'd say, 'If you think I'm competitive, you should see the Mallorys.'"

Such competitiveness produced winning results, even against Big Ten superpowers such as Ohio State and Michigan. In one four-year stretch, the Hoosiers were 2–1–1 against the Buckeyes, and it could have been more. They pushed the Wolverines to the limit.

"It was the first time when Indiana fans went into games against Michigan and Ohio State where they thought Indiana had a chance to win," Hammel said. "They were within reach.

"There was a four-year period where they could have gone 4–0 versus Ohio State. They did win two. Indiana blew the Buckeyes out here [41–7 in 1988] after winning 31–10 at Ohio State in 1987.

"They had a pep rally here [in 1988], and Bill takes out a buckeye and stomps on it. I thought, *Oh my God*. Indiana led 34–0 at half-time. Anthony had tied the IU touchdown record at halftime.

"The next year over there [1989], IU was the better team. It came down to the last five minutes. Ohio State was up by six. They took a safety and got a free kick. They punted it and recovered it. They got to keep the ball and ran out the clock.

"They would not have stopped Anthony Thompson at the end of that game. I remember an Ohio State defensive back squared up to tackle Anthony. You watch the film, and all of a sudden, the defensive back is no longer on the film. Anthony had knocked him clear out of camera range and scored the touchdown."

Then came a 27–27 tie with the Buckeyes in 1990. Thompson was gone, and future All-American tailback Vaughn Dunbar had replaced him. Dunbar scored an apparent touchdown that would have put IU ahead late in the game, but officials called a penalty. No touchdown. The Hoosiers would settle for a field goal and a tie.

"It was that kind of Ohio State-Michigan-Michigan State call that always seemed to go against Indiana," Hammel said. "There was no way the penalty had anything to do with that touchdown."

Bad breaks remain an unwanted part of IU football tradition. But in the Mallory era, they were kept to a minimum as he built a program that emphasized doing the right things the right way.

"With Bill, Indiana continued to build," Fischer said. "It was a slow process. It wasn't overnight. It took them three years to go to a bowl. That kind of progress solidified him and his staff as guys who could build."

And so they did.

⤍═◉═⤏

Understanding how Mallory thrived at Indiana means understanding his recruiting.

"We got into the areas we focused on and worked it hard," Mallory says. "High school coaches had good respect for us. We'd go into Ohio. People would ask, 'Why are you recruiting in Ohio? How are you going to beat out Ohio State, Notre Dame, or Michigan?'

"I'd say, 'I'm not. Let them take theirs. We'll take the others. We got some darn good ones there.'"

That included walk-ons.

"I really pushed on walk-ons, particularly in state," Mallory says. "I want to mention one—Joe Huff. He was one of the better players we had."

Mallory was hired in mid-January of 1984, basically two weeks before signing day. In other words, it seemed like a lost recruiting class. It was not.

"After [signing day], my secretary came in and said, 'There's a mother—Mary Jo Huff— and her son, Joe, here. They want to talk to you.'"

Mallory laughs at the memory.

"You have to know Mary Jo. She has her jaw locked. She is a wonderful woman. Her husband, Bill, was great, but he was more laidback. She was a fiery gal. She sat down, pointed at me, and said, 'You made a mistake. You didn't recruit my son, Joe.'

"I said, 'Well, we probably made a lot of mistakes.' She said, 'He'll walk on here, and if you don't want him, we'll go see [head coach] Earle Bruce at Ohio State.'

"Earle and I are good friends. We were on staff at Ohio State. I said, 'You don't need to go any further. Joe can stay here, and I'll treat him fair and square. If he shows he can play, I'll scholarship him.'"

Huff had been a standout player for Castle High School's powerhouse program but had fallen under the recruiting radar. It didn't take long to realize that the radar had malfunctioned.

"He came in, and I saw right away he was going to be a player," Mallory says. "I had a scholarship and gave it to him midyear as a freshman."

Huff went on to earn first-team All-Big Ten honors as a senior linebacker/defensive end in 1989 and rivaled more heralded defensive teammate Van Waiters for game-changing impact.

"Van was a darn good player who went on to a good pro career," Mallory says. "I wanted to put up both for the All-Big Ten. The other coaches said, 'Waiters is a darn good player, but that mother [bleeping] little guy on the other side can really play.' Joe could run with anybody. He was one tough guy to block."

Huff, and other walk-ons, made huge contributions to Mallory's program-building efforts.

"They all helped to put together a team."

Still, walk-ons could only do so much in the ultracompetitive Big Ten. You needed dominant players, and it started, Mallory says, with finding guys he could count on.

"What I really looked hard at was character and attitude," Mallory says. "First and foremost, I didn't want any bums. Not that I didn't have a few I had to put the thumb on. We looked at potential. The coaches worked with the players. They grew up, matured, and developed. I tried to redshirt freshmen. Give them a chance to grow up and go from there."

More than any other freshman under Mallory, tailback Anthony Thompson didn't need a redshirt season. He was strong, powerful, and fierce coming out of nearby Terre Haute.

"He was ready to play right away," Mallory says.

An injury kept Thompson out of the first four games. In his first game, against Wisconsin, he rushed for 207 yards.

"From that point on," Mallory says, "he never missed a game."

Thompson was the 1989 Heisman Trophy runner-up and finished with a then-NCAA record 67 touchdowns and a school-record 5,299 career yards. Thompson personified Mallory's in-state emphasis. He had a staff of strong recruiters, led by recruiting coordinator Jim Muehling, but it went beyond that, Mallory says.

"You also had to look at the wives. They were very involved in recruiting. Jim was a heck of a recruiter. He was our best. His wife, Bevo, might have been the next best. We had a family atmosphere."

Like every coach, Mallory targeted in-state players. Unlike every Hoosier coach, he backed it up.

"I did not think they had done a good enough job in this state," he says. "In fact, we got some players from that Gary area, which was pretty quality football. It was very good. Why in the world wouldn't Indiana be on them?"

Mallory raises his arms like a ref signaling a touchdown.

"I told our coaches we were going to hit every place that had a goal post. We were going to hit this entire state. So don't you miss one!"

He jabs a finger for emphasis.

"We were going to hit it throughout, and we did."

Mallory got high school coaches to come to IU for practice. He and his staff conducted statewide clinics for prep coaches.

"We got together with them. We developed a good rapport with them. I developed such a respect for Indiana high school football. I didn't feel it was given the credit it deserved. Purdue was doing a better job recruiting in state than we were at the start, and I told the coaches we're going to make sure Purdue doesn't out-recruit us.

"We got a lot of productivity out of in-state recruiting. That's where it started."

Award-winning radio announcer Don Fischer saw firsthand how hard IU coaches worked the state and the payoff that resulted.

"High school coaches bought into it," Fischer says. "Bill spoke to all the high school teams. He and his staff went to all these golf outings all over the state, fifteen a year, and got the fans involved and the alumni believing that this guy cares about Indiana. There was a buy-in from everybody because of how Bill handled himself. When you heard him speak, you heard a guy who had passion, emotion, toughness, and, more than anything else, respect. He had respect for the program, and that respect was given back to him.

"That buy-in was the difference in why the program became successful under him."

IU's success depended on more than Indiana high school players, so Mallory and his staff, just as Tom Allen and his staff do now, went to nearby states such as Ohio, Michigan, Illinois, and Kentucky and then branched out for selective national recruiting.

"Jim Muehling was one of the best recruiters I've ever been around," Mallory says. "He had good contacts. I just turned him loose. He went out East and got players. He had a good feel of where to go outside of our main territory in the Midwest.

"We'd spot recruit Florida, particularly for skills players. We got some good skill players there.

"I did not hit junior colleges very hard unless there was an area we needed to beef up. I wanted to make sure he was a good, quality person. [Offensive lineman] Eric Moore was a good example. He came in from Missouri and went on to be an All-America and have a good pro career."

Standout players under Mallory included quarterbacks Dave Schnell and Trent Green; receivers Ernie Jones and Thomas Lewis; running backs Anthony Thompson and Vaughn Dunbar; offensive linemen Andrew Greene, Ron Vargo, Don Shrader, and Ian Beckles; tight end Rod Coleman; kickers Pete Stoyanovich, Scott Bonnell, and Bill Manolopolos; defensive linemen Hurvin McCormack and John Hammerstein; linebackers Mark Hagen, Joe Fitzgerald, Joe Huff, and Van Waiters; defensive backs Mike Dumas and Eric Allen; and punters Jim DiGuilio and Macky Smith.

Ernie Jones rates as one of the best receivers in IU history. He was the Associated Press player of the year in 1987 after catching 66 passes for 13 touchdowns and a school season receiving yards record of 1,265. He totaled 1,807 all-purpose yards. He went on to play six seasons in the NFL.

"Ernie was a real impact player," Mallory says. "He was as fine a receiver as I ever had to be around and to coach. He was just such a great playmaker. He had that toughness and talent you need as a receiver. When you threw Ernie the ball, you know it was going to be, most times, caught."

Beyond that, Mallory credits a strong academic support staff.

"I inherited a great academic staff with Buzz Kurpius. They were outstanding. It wasn't a spoon-feeding situation. We were very focused on academics. I expected players to be in class, and they were."

⋆⇒◉⇐⋆

Understanding how Mallory thrived at Indiana means understanding how he became a Hoosier. Basketball coach Bob Knight played a huge role.

Mallory had been a tough-as-nails football player at Miami of Ohio who honed his coaching philosophy as an assistant coach at Bowling Green, Yale, and Ohio State. He became the head coach at Miami of Ohio in 1969 and in five seasons never won fewer than seven games while going 39–12. In his final season, in 1973, Miami went 11–0 and won the Mid-American Conference title and then the Tangerine Bowl.

Then Mallory moved to Colorado. In five seasons, his teams went 35–21–1 and had winning records in his last four years. In 1975, the Buffaloes went 9–3. The next season, they were 8–4–1 and won the Big Eight championship. But after a seventh-place conference finish in 1978, he was let go and spent a year out of coaching.

Then came a four-year run at Northern Illinois, highlighted by the 1983 Mid-American Conference title. The Huskies were 10–2 and won the California Bowl. His record there was 25–19.

Meanwhile, Indiana was in a football mess. The Hoosiers had fired coach Lee Corso in 1982 after his 41–68–2 run and replaced him with offensive innovator Sam Wyche, who had helped the San Francisco 49ers win the Super Bowl. But he lasted only one season before leaving to take over the NFL's Cincinnati Bengals.

That devastated recruiting, continuity, and more. IU needed someone who could bring stability and success to the program. Someone who knew how to build a winner. Someone, as it turned out, like Bill Mallory.

"We had just come back from the California Bowl when I was at Northern Illinois," Mallory says. "I get this call. He said, 'It's Bob Knight.' I didn't know him well. I knew him a little from [Michigan football coach Bo Schembechler] and [Ohio State coach Woody Hayes]. They were all good friends. So he said, 'This is Bob Knight.' You know how Bob could be. He got right to the point. 'Are you interested in the Indiana job?'"

Mallory's first reaction: this was a joke.

"I thought, *Is someone setting me up here?* Then as we talked, I recognized that this is who it had to be. He said Sam had left and was going to the Bengals. I said, 'I am interested if Indiana will make a commitment to football.' He said they are. He said they have an excellent athletic director in Ralph Floyd. Ralph had been a football coach. He'd been in the arena. He understood.

"Ralph and I talked. He said, 'I'm going to hire you.' I said, 'Good.' I was able to bring in my staff from Northern Illinois, knowing that it was going to be challenging."

In fact, it was a huge challenge, starting with recruiting. Three head coaches in three years was no way to build a program.

Mallory and the Hoosiers made the most of it even though the 0–11 first-season record didn't reflect that. Or did it?

"What always stood out with me was his 0–11 season," Bob Hammel says. "You'd think that would make you think, *This guy can't make it*, but that's what convinced me he would. It was how hard they played. He kept them through all that. They kept losing tight games. They lost every way you could lose."

The Hoosiers lost eight games by nine or fewer points while learning to play the Mallory way. That meant strong fundamentals and hard, aggressive play. The only blowout losses came against Kentucky, 48–14, and Ohio State, 50–7. IU lost to a good Wisconsin team 20–16, to No. 14 Michigan 14–6, and then to Purdue 31–24.

"Purdue was a much better team," Hammel says, "but Indiana jumped out 14–0. [The Hoosiers] came at them. Wisconsin had, like, ten guys get drafted. They were really good, and Indiana played them right down to the wire."

In fact, the Hoosiers were positioned to win. Freshman receiver Ernie Jones, just starting an All-Big Ten career, was to get the ball on a reverse. The play was set up perfectly. A touchdown seemed a certainty along with a potential victory.

Except . . .

"The Wisconsin cornerback blitzed, and the linebacker fell," Hammel says. "They'd taken themselves completely out of the play.

"Indiana had seven guys coming around [to block]. Wisconsin had one guy back. Bill says, 'I'd like to have thought we'd have gotten that guy.' It couldn't have been a more perfect setup. He's going to waltz in, but the exchange was dropped. The running back handing off to Jones lost it."

Hammel pauses and thinks about Mallory's postgame comment and laughs.

"'I'd like to think we'd have gotten that guy,' he said."

In the aftermath, Mallory found perspective.

"To reflect back, where I was so proud of that team even though it lost all eleven games was that of the nine Big Ten teams we played, [six] were within a touchdown or less. We were competitive, but we couldn't get it finished. Two teams kicked our rumps pretty good, one being Ohio State, which fired me up because I had coached there. I said, 'We'll get those guys down the road.'"

That first season set a foundation for future success.

"The thing Bill did that first year and that everybody respected," long-time voice of the Hoosiers, radio announcer Don Fischer, says, "was that everybody who ever played for him had respect for him. He didn't throw those kids under the bus because they weren't his recruits. He got those kids to buy in to what he was selling.

"He said, 'This will be the hardest thing you've ever done. We didn't recruit you, but we're asking you to lay the foundation for a program that we think will be special.' Those kids believed him and bought into it.

"Even though that team didn't win a game, you could feel the change and what he was doing from a coaching perspective. Just having the kids believe in what they were doing. You could feel it. It was obvious in every game they played. They just couldn't find a way to win."

The Hoosiers would eventually find that way. That first team set the foundation for future success.

"We honored those guys," Mallory says. "I told them at the end, 'Don't reflect on the 0–11 record; reflect on your focus and the way you worked hard.' I didn't have to get on them about hanging heads or pointing fingers. Those guys came out and busted tail. Maybe they weren't quite good enough, maybe we could have coached them better, but we just weren't quite where we needed to be at the Big Ten level."

IU went 4–7 the next season and then 6–5 in 1986, good enough to play in the All-American Bowl in Birmingham, Alabama. It was just the Hoosiers' third bowl in school history. They lost to Florida State 27–13, but it set a tone. Indiana was no longer a patsy.

"The second year we got a little better and won four games," Mallory says, "but we still didn't make the progress I wanted to see.

"The third year we had a lot of guys we had brought in. They'd matured and were upper-class level. We were able to get a winning season and go to a bowl. The next year we were able to come up with a good degree of success."

The real breakthrough came in 1987, when the Hoosiers went 8–4 and finished second in the Big Ten. They had two stunning victories: at No. 9 Ohio State, 31–10, and over No. 20 Michigan, 14–10.

Their big gun was sophomore tailback Anthony Thompson, who would rush for 1,014 yards and 12 touchdowns.

They had a chance to win the Big Ten title. They faced Michigan State in East Lansing in mid-November with a big opportunity, but it would come without injured starting quarterback Dave Schnell. IU fell behind early and never challenged in a 27–3 defeat.

"That season really introduced Anthony Thompson as a top back in the country," Hammel says. "Indiana beat Ohio State and Michigan. They went to Michigan State with a chance to go to the Rose Bowl and got blown out. I don't think they could have beaten Michigan State, but it would have been a lot different game if Dave Schnell had been there."

The Hoosiers came back to beat Purdue 35–14 to finish with a 6–2 Big Ten record. They lost to Tennessee in the Peach Bowl.

The next season, IU went 8–3–1, 5–3 in the Big Ten, crushed Purdue 52–7, and beat South Carolina 34–10 in the Liberty Bowl.

In 1989, the Hoosiers were positioned to make a fourth straight bowl game. All they had to do was beat a struggling Purdue team in the regular season finale at Memorial Stadium. Trailing 15–14, they had a chance to win in the final seconds with a field goal. The field goal was missed, the game was lost, and the opportunity was over. They finished 5–6.

IU went 6–5 and 7–4 the next two seasons with Trent Green as the quarterback. It lost to Auburn 27–23 in the 1990 Peach Bowl and beat Baylor 24–0 in the 1991 Copper Bowl.

The Hoosiers had a chance to make a bowl in 1992 but lost their last three games, including a 13–10 heartbreaker at Purdue.

Indiana opened strong in 1993. It won seven of its first eight games, including consecutive shutouts over Northwestern and Michigan State. It lost by seven points to No. 18 Penn State and by six points to No. 5 Ohio State, both on the road.

The Hoosiers beat Purdue 24–17 and were positioned for another bowl game. The destination—the Independence Bowl in Shreveport, Louisiana—didn't excite the fan base. Neither did the result: a 45–20 loss to No. 21 Virginia Tech.

Still, Indiana finished 8–4 and tied for fourth in the Big Ten. Everything seemed positioned for the Hoosiers to win for the foreseeable future.

Then things got complicated.

⊷⊜⊜⊷

Flash back to 1994. IU started 5–1 then lost four straight, including six-point losses to Michigan State and No. 2 Penn State. The Hoosiers won at Purdue 33–29 to finish 6–5. Motor City Bowl officials came calling to offer a bid. IU athlete officials turned it down.

Here's Mallory's view: "That fires me up," he says. "That team was good enough to go, but we just would not make a commitment here. That's when it got irking. We lost [athletic director] Ralph Floyd. He had passed away. I didn't feel the commitment was quite there.

"That 1994 team was good enough to go. The Motor City Bowl [located in Detroit] wanted us. I would have gone. We recruited Michigan. We got some good young men out of Michigan. So the Motor City Bowl wanted us, but [IU officials] didn't feel it would pay off enough. They were going to have to pay a little bit. It wasn't that big a deal. We had some other bowls that expressed interest, but the Motor City was a firm offer. I liked those people. I can't believe we wouldn't have taken that opportunity. All bowls were good."

After the season, Michigan State had to forfeit all its victories, so IU's final official record was 7–4.

The magic faded the next two seasons. The Hoosiers went 2–9 and 3–8, winning just one of sixteen Big Ten games. Attendance fell. Fan apathy grew.

Mallory had one more year left on his contract and wanted to finish it. He believed he could turn things around, especially with future superstar quarterback Antwaan Randle El coming the next season (1997). As it turned out, Randle El was academically ineligible and didn't play until 1998.

Mallory never got the chance for a turnaround. IU officials announced a few weeks before the 1996 season ended that this would be his final season.

Mallory went out a winner—beating Purdue at Ross-Ade Stadium 33–16 in his final game as a head coach.

"At the end, he ran into some difficulties, some key injuries," Hammel says. "They weren't deep enough to afford that. He really wanted to coach Randle El. He wanted one more year. He thought he'd get it going again with Randle El. As it turned out, Antwaan wasn't eligible.

"I was never pleased with the way [Mallory's firing] went down. The wrong people were making that choice. It was the guys in the stands second guessing and giving big money thinking they could run a football team. They didn't know how to run a football team.

"They said, 'I could call the next play—it will be tailback off tackle.' Well, that tailback was an All-American—Anthony Thompson. O. J. Simpson ran off tackle too. It was nonsense to second guess what was going on."

Don Fischer also didn't like the way IU treated Mallory then and still doesn't.

"My biggest issues were with how people felt at the end of his reign," Fischer says. "It wasn't good enough to go to the Weed Eater Bowl or the Peach Bowl or the Liberty Bowl or Copper Bowl. Those weren't good enough. They wanted to go to the Rose Bowl, the Orange Bowl, and the Sugar Bowl. I understand that. You want to make that upgrade. But it's hard for a program like Indiana to do that.

"There was such malice in some people's minds: 'We're not going to this place or that place. It's not good enough.' That made me sick. It made me hurt for the whole program. You have to be happy for what you got. What you wish for, you might not get, or you might get something a lot worse than what you got."

After Mallory left, IU didn't make a bowl for eleven seasons, and that was with having one of the best Big Ten quarterbacks ever in Randle El for three years. Mallory was angry, but not bitter, and still came to IU games and practices. He's convinced Allen will deliver a consistent winner.

"Tom is on track. He knows what he's doing. His coaches know what they're doing. The big thing with Tom is he's very focused and positive. I go to practice. I see it. He's into it. Sure, he gets after players with tough love, firmness. What he's doing is right. I feel so confident in what they're doing here. I feel they'll continually get better.

"I told Tom, 'Keep doing what you're doing. It will pay dividends down the road.'"

⊷⊜⊶

Mallory never saw those dividends. He died in May 2018 at the age of eighty-two, and during a Celebration of Life, former players, coaches, and more came to Memorial Stadium to honor him one last time.

The funeral service at First United Methodist Church in downtown Bloomington drew so many the overflow was held at nearby Buskirk Chumley Theater.

Stories were told by some of those Mallory most inspired. They detail his passion, dedication, and determination to always—always—live up to the highest standards.

"Coach Mal spoke with passion," Anthony Thompson says. "He was a man of great conviction. He cared about each and every one of us. It was great to know him."

Mark Hagen met Mallory thirty years earlier as a heralded recruit out of Carmel High School near Indianapolis. He became an All-Big Ten IU player and then a college coach. He's now the Hoosiers' defensive line coach and assistant defensive coordinator, and continues to follow Mallory's do-it-right example.

"Bill Mallory was a man of honesty and integrity," Hagan says. "He never minced words. You always knew where you stood.

"It was tough playing for Coach Mal, but life is tough. We'd run through a brick wall for him."

Hagen recalls a 1989 practice when the defense was struggling so badly, Mallory decided to show his players how to tackle. He went after future All-America tailback Vaughn Dunbar and wound up with broken glasses, a busted watch, and a cut above his eye.

"His competitiveness was off the charts," Hagen says. "He demanded toughness."

Those demands paid off.

IU had just five winning seasons in the thirty-six years before Mallory's 1983 arrival. It has had just one since he was fired in 1996. He had six winning records in his thirteen seasons.

"That tells you all you need to know about Bill Mallory," Fischer says.

But beyond that, Fischer adds, "The real legacy of Bill Mallory was not the winning or losing or the many honors, but the lives he touched and the way he lived his extraordinary life."

CHAPTER 11

# Lee Corso

LEE CORSO COMES, SEES, CONQUERS.

Of course he does.

Yes, the ESPN *College GameDay* icon and former Indiana football coach moves a little slower, speaks a little softer. Pauses break up sentences. The one-time rush of words comes in measured doses. The unforgiving one-two punch of age and a stroke rocked Corso but didn't break him. He's too tough for that.

"The fans keep me energized, and the GameDay crew is the best medicine for an old coach," he says.

Corso arrives in Bloomington for two reasons in late August of 2017: to receive the Bill Orwig Award, given to a non-alumnus who has made major contributions to IU athletics, and to work the Indiana-Ohio State game for GameDay.

Rest and naps are key to his longevity. Time gets the best of everyone in the end, but Corso, well into his eighties, battles on—to hell with retirement talk.

"Why would I want to retire?" Corso famously asks. "I'm having too much fun."

Fun follows Corso. ESPN colleagues vouch to that.

"Lee is a humble man," ESPN GameDay announcer Rece Davis says. "He's the heartbeat of the show. Everything is built around him. He's more responsible for the chemistry on that set than anybody. As he reminds us all the time, 'It's entertainment, sweetheart.'"

The humor, resolve, and passion that highlighted Corso's ten-year run at Indiana are as strong as ever. He showcases that, and more, from an elevated table at Bloomington's Holiday Inn Express during a late-morning media gathering hours before the season-opening IU-Ohio State game.

"This has been amazing for me," he says. "I never had an idea, when I was doing those TV shows in Indianapolis, that I could end up doing this."

A pause.

"I can't say enough about Indiana giving me a chance to come here and ESPN especially. During my career, ESPN could have dumped me, but they didn't."

His eyes moisten from emotion.

"I appreciate what they've done."

The reinvention of Corso from standout athlete (he was once so fast as a Florida State football player that he was known as the "Sunshine Scooter") to entertaining coach to ESPN TV icon still inspires. When the idea surfaced to bring *College GameDay* to Bloomington for the first time ever in the spring of 2017, everyone was on board.

"We all have such affection for [Corso]," Davis says, "that when we saw this opportunity, we were like, 'Let's go.'"

So they did.

Corso is the heart and soul of GameDay, and the crew treats him as such. Kirk Herbstreit, Desmond Howard, David Pollack, and Davis are there when he stumbles and forever have his back. His return to broadcasting four months after his 2009 stroke—thanks to intensive therapy and help from his ESPN co-workers—reflects the best of their camaraderie.

"Truth be told, he's like the czar of the sport, not the ruling czar or heavy handed but one who has influence, who evokes great affection," Davis says. "He is a huge part of the show."

Davis suggests that if the College Football Hall of Fame ever gets a section for contributors, Corso should top the list.

"Who has contributed more in terms of the popularity of the sport?" Davis says. "Who has done more than Lee Corso? His spot is firmly established. He's one of the great entertainers in the history of the game on TV and one of the outstanding coaches who translated more seamlessly to the TV side than anybody I can think of."

Corso's coaching and broadcasting accomplishments followed impressive athletic achievements. The son of Italian immigrants, he was a multisport high school standout in Florida, playing quarterback in football, guard in basketball, and shortstop in baseball at Miami Jackson. At his father's insistence, he turned down a $5,000 baseball signing bonus with the then Brooklyn Dodgers to play football at Florida State, and his roommate was Burt Reynolds, who later became the world's number-one movie star.

The speedy Corso played quarterback, receiver, running back, and defensive back for the Seminoles. He had games where, at different times, he led the team in passing, rushing, receiving, kick returns, punt returns, and interceptions. His 14 career interceptions set a school record, later broken by eventual NFL Hall of Famer Deion Sanders.

Impressive? Sure, but it's not the reason he returned to Bloomington.

It had been thirty-five years since Corso had last watched an Indiana game at Memorial Stadium—which was the one he coached, a 48–7 loss to Illinois. Before the IU-Ohio State game, he met with most members of his former coaching staff. Later, he reunited with more than a hundred former players.

What does Corso think of current coach Tom Allen's prospects for Hoosier success?

"Tom is a terrific guy. The team was excited about him being named coach. I think it was a great move to name him coach. He has all the state contacts. His father coached at [New Castle]. He has the background to be a great coach here.

"To win, you've got to get players. You win with good players. That's no secret. You have to keep recruiting and keep winning. The most important thing is don't prostitute your integrity to get those players. You never lose your integrity to win. Do it the right way. That's the secret."

Corso did it the right way, and if it didn't always produce the hoped-for number of victories (he was 73–85–6 as a college head coach, 5–13 in his one season for Orlando in the long-gone United States Football League), well, you can't always get what you want.

Take his departure from Indiana. Corso was recruiting at Fort Wayne Snider High School—trying to land future NFL Hall of Famer Rod Woodson—when his wife called to tell him newspapers were reporting that he had been fired.

"It about destroyed me," he later said.

It did not, of course. If anything, it toughened him even more. Indiana appeared in just one bowl game under Corso, but it was among the most memorable ever played, a 38–37 thriller over previously unbeaten Brigham Young in the 1979 Holiday Bowl. The Hoosiers finished 8–4 and earned their first top-twenty ranking since their Rose Bowl season of 1967.

Some saw Corso in coach-as-clown terms. They found negativity given he produced losing records in eight of his ten Hoosier years, winning just 41 games overall. But that missed his point, which was that football was entertainment as much as sport, and especially given Indiana's historical struggles in the sport, you might as well have fun while you played. No coach had more fun than Corso.

In 1976, after IU scored a touchdown to take an early 7–6 lead over powerhouse Ohio State, Corso called a timeout and gathered his team so they could take a team photo with the scoreboard in the background as proof the Hoosiers had their first lead over the Buckeyes in twenty-five years.

Then there was his weekly in-season TV show. During one hilarious opening bit after a tough loss, he emerged in a coffin, only to pop up and say into the camera, "We ain't dead yet!"

"When I was at Indiana, I had terrific TV shows," Corso says with a laugh. "I had bad teams but terrific TV shows."

That followed a successful Louisville run, during which Corso once rode an elephant in a parade to promote the program and even used a turkey as an inspirational mascot against heavily favored

Tulsa. It worked. Louisville won, and the team carried Corso and the turkey off the field in celebration.

That humorous approach continued during his thirty-year-plus run at ESPN (he was hired in 1987 as a contributor, then became an analyst) when he entertained by spiking fish; putting on mascot heads; delivering his famous line, "No so fast, my friend," while flashing a No. 2 pencil as a prop (showing good business sense, Corso joined pencil manufacturer Dixon Ticonderoga as director of business development); or even uttering the one word you can't say on TV (as was once documented during comedian George Carlin's famous bit).

He apologized, moved on, and never forgot the opportunity ESPN gave him.

"I can say a lot of things about ESPN, and people say a lot of things about ESPN, but a couple of years ago, they could have gotten rid of me. They could have dumped me. I had my stroke and couldn't talk. They stayed with me. They gave me a chance to get back."

A pause.

"They changed my schedule a little bit. I'm not on the road all the time. I get a chance to rest. If I don't rest, I can't talk."

Corso is talking now. In a few hours, he will receive that Orwig Award. It's named after the former Indiana athletic director who hired him in the early 1970s. He will work the game against Ohio State, get some needed rest, and then work the season-opening epic two days later between No. 1 Alabama and No. 3 Florida State.

He will fly first class, stay at a nice hotel, eat good meals, and get to do what he forever loves. Along the way, he will:

Come.

See.

Conquer.

⋅►══◐ ◑══◄⋅

Holiday Bowl.

It was seven years in the making, this bowl opportunity.

Corso had arrived pushing a victory promise in 1972, and in 1979, after a seemingly never-ending series of tough losses and near misses, it finally came true. With players such as quarterback Tim Clifford (the Big Ten MVP after throwing for 2,078 yards and 13 touchdowns), running backs Lonnie Johnson and Mike Harkrader, tight end Bob Stephenson, and cornerback Tim Wilbur, the Hoosiers found glory where few outside the program expected.

They opened the season 3–0 with wins over Iowa, Vanderbilt, and Kentucky and just missed making it 4–0. They lost to Colorado 17–16.

IU finished with a 7–4 regular season record and earned a berth in the Holiday Bowl in San Diego, California. The opponent was unbeaten Brigham Young, an offensive powerhouse behind record-setting quarterback Marc Wilson, who led the nation in passing and total offense.

Cougar fans thought they deserved a more prestigious opponent to fit their top-ten national ranking and booed when the Hoosiers were selected. Then the game started, and Wilson went to work. He would throw for 380 yards and 2 touchdowns. However, IU also intercepted him three times.

Clifford threw for 171 yards and a touchdown. Johnson rushed for 76 yards. Harkrader added 71. The Hoosiers jumped ahead 14–7 in the first quarter and 21–17 at halftime. Clifford accounted for all the scoring, twice on 1-yard touchdown runs, once on a 38-yard TD pass to Stephenson.

Brigham Young's 17-point third-quarter burst gave them a 34–31 lead. The Cougars added an early fourth-quarter field goal to make it 37–31.

With eight minutes left, Brigham Young punted, and the ball hit IU's Craig Walls on the back and bounced to a surprised Wilbur, who took advantage by returning it 62 yards for a touchdown to tie the score. Kevin Kellogg's extra point put the Hoosiers ahead 38–37.

Brigham Young had one last chance and drove into field goal range. With seven seconds left, kicker Brent Johnson eyed a 27-yard attempt. He already was 3-for-3 in the game, including one from 46 yards.

This time, he missed. Brigham Young was unbeaten no more. And the Hoosiers had their first-ever bowl victory.

"It's a great win for the Big Ten," Corso said in a postgame press conference after the game, according to Doug Robinson of the *Deseret News*. "If BYU's number nine, then we're eighth."

IU won despite trailing in total yards (520 to 354) and first downs (31 to 21). However, the Hoosiers did have the ball ten more minutes than the Cougars, which was part of the game plan.

"If it goes into a shootout," Corso said in a pregame press conference, according to the *Deseret News*, "we'll get killed. We might come out in a basketball stall."

Instead, Indiana won a shootout, and in the aftermath, Corso, who had delivered a series of entertaining press conferences leading up to the game, turned serious.

"I hope people wonder about inviting Indiana now," he said in the *Deseret News*. "Don't forget that a certain amount of humor is not a sign of weakness. We came here to win."

And so the Hoosiers did.

## CHAPTER 12

# Rose Bowl Glory

KEN KACZMAREK WAS THERE, AND HE WASN'T. PHYSICALLY, he sat at a table in Bloomington restaurant C3 in the fall of 2017 as part of a reception for the fiftieth anniversary of Indiana's 1967 Rose Bowl team. Mentally and emotionally, he was back in Pasadena during that 1968 glory opportunity, a hard-hitting All-American senior linebacker about to experience the best athletic moment of his life.

But first Kaczmarek went back six weeks further, to mid-November of 1967, to a game at Michigan State in front of seventy-one thousand Spartan fans.

He was asked what his favorite memory of that season was. You might have expected it to be the Purdue game, a victory he helped save with a ferocious tackle of Boiler fullback Perry Williams. The hit forced Williams to fumble inside the IU 5-yard line. The Hoosiers recovered to end the Boilers' last real scoring chance.

It was not his favorite.

Kaczmarek's best memory was beating Michigan State 14–13 to pay back a 37–19 loss to the No. 2 Spartans the previous season.

"My junior year they devastated us," he said. "They wrecked Kevin Duffy's spleen. They separated Gary Tofil's shoulder. Tom Schuette broke his hand. Bill Couch, a great split end, hurt his knee.

"We remembered that. So we went up there to kill Michigan State. I'm serious. Kill them. We wanted to kill them."

Kaczmarek smiled without warmth.

"And we did."

For the record, Kaczmarek did not mean the actual taking of life but to pound the Spartans into submission. And while the score didn't show submission, the thrill of victory made up for it. For Kaczmarek, nothing thrilled better than defense. His 118 tackles as a senior ranked second in the Big Ten and highlighted a quest to perform at the highest level. Although an all-state high school player at powerhouse South Bend St. Joseph's, he didn't draw much interest from nearby Notre Dame. Idaho State, Wyoming, and Kansas State were very interested. So were Navy, Northwestern, Purdue, and Indiana.

Navy was his favorite, but he didn't pass the physical. The Hoosiers offered the best chance to play early, plus had a strong business school. That was important because Kaczmarek wanted to pursue a business career.

He signed with IU and coach Phil Dickens but played for Pont after Dickens was fired. Kaczmarek excelled as much because of his passion as for his ability, and Michigan State faced the full force of that emotion during the Hoosiers' Rose Bowl run.

The Spartan offense couldn't do anything against IU defensive coordinator Ernie Plank's fired-up Hoosiers. Indiana held on for that 1-point victory—Kaczmarek sealed it with a late interception— to improve to 8–0, tying the school record for the longest winning streak set by the 1945 Big Ten champs.

"Our defense played one of the best games any IU defense has ever played," Kaczmarek said. "That's my biggest memory. Michigan State got the ball on the 4-yard line in the second quarter [off a Hoosier turnover] and ended up on the 6-yard line because we blitzed them three different ways, and they had no idea what we were doing."

Michigan State settled for a field goal.

Kaczmarek smiled again. He had emotionally returned to 2017, but that 9–2 season that included eight wins decided in the final four minutes, seven by a touchdown or less, remained as vivid as a bolt of lightning.

"We had a lot of experience, brashness, and quickness other teams didn't have," he said.

Around him, former teammates mingled. Time had done its work. They were no longer young and bulletproof, but they had the memories and the friendships, and that made all the difference. "It doesn't seem like a half century ago," Kaczmarek said. "Everybody moved on with their lives, and most have been very successful." Kaczmarek reflected that success. He became executive director of the Indiana Port Commission, a member of the American Institute of Certified Public Accountants, and the chief economic officer for Peloton Wealth Strategists, a successful investment management company. He also continues to give back to the university that has meant so much to him.

But on this night, nothing mattered except Rose Bowl glory. "You know what?" he said. "It was a lot of fun."

⋆⟶⟾◉⟸⟵⋆

Eric Stolberg was there, and he wasn't. He, too, was at C3—he's a part owner through his WS Property Group development business—for the Rose Bowl reception that was broadcast on Bloomington radio station WGCL AM-1370 and hosted by WCGL's Mike Glasscott and Dave Novak. However, Stolberg also was flashing back to the season when Indiana shocked the college football world.

Now he's a hugely successful real estate developer, Bloomington community leader, and IU contributor. Then, he was a standout wide receiver, not in the manner of touchdown-scoring All-American teammate Jade Butcher, but good enough to make a difference. He was fast and tough and driven to succeed. And so he did.

Stolberg was tough enough to play through multiple dislocated shoulders—he said it was thirty—during that Rose Bowl season because, well, why not? He saw what the outside world didn't see— these Hoosiers were not the perennial patsies of the previous twenty years. They would do something special, and he wasn't about to miss out.

The secret of their success, as it turned out, wasn't so secret.

"We had a dynamic sophomore class," Stolberg said. "There were a bunch of talented, brash, cocky guys on offense that melded really well with a strong senior class. The combination of those two dynamics allowed us to win."

Win but not dominate. Victory came by staying in the moment.

"We didn't look ahead at all," Stolberg said. "We won a lot by one, two, three points. We were taking those games one at a time. The more we won, the more confident we became and the more trust we had with each other.

"We built that momentum. It wasn't, 'Maybe we'll win,' it was, 'We're going to win. We don't know how, but we're going to win.'"

That belief started with coach John Pont. He'd won at Miami of Ohio and then at Yale before coming to Indiana. He didn't come to Bloomington to lose. Neither did Stolberg.

Stolberg once seemed destined for track glory. He was a dominant hurdler coming out of Cuyahoga Falls High School in Ohio, good enough to have Olympic dreams. Ohio State and Michigan State offered track scholarships and said he could play football if he wanted.

He wanted. The twist: football was his top priority. That put other schools that had offered football scholarships—IU, North Carolina, Northwestern, and Miami of Ohio—into play.

Only the Hoosiers had the Pont recruiting advantage.

"I can tell you what Coach Pont told me when I was being recruited," Stolberg said. "In his office, he gave me this firm look and said, 'I want you to come to Indiana and help us go to the Rose Bowl because that's where we want to go and that's where we're going to go.'"

That IU had never gone to the Rose Bowl was of no importance to Pont, or to Stolberg, or to any of the players who joined the cream 'n' crimson cause.

"I believed him," Stolberg said. "I had multiple offers to go elsewhere, and I came to Indiana."

Coming meant saying no to Indiana track coach Sam Bell, a Hall of Famer who wanted Stolberg to run hurdles in the spring. But

Stolberg didn't want to miss football spring practice, so there would be no hurdling.

There would be plenty of Pont fire.

"He was intense," Stolberg said. "Very intense. He was a good guy. He backed his players to the max. He expected a lot out of you."

Pont got a lot, Kaczmarek added. "Coach Pont was fiery, intense, and competitive. There was something about him that he hated to lose."

That intensity surfaced in the 1967 season-opening game against Kentucky. The Hoosiers trailed 10–0 at halftime. Pont was so angry in the locker room, he kicked the film projector. IU went on to win 12–10. That set a hard-hitting tone—and spurred a beast of a defense that held nine opponents to 20 or fewer points.

Amid the winning, players sometimes chose the path less followed. For instance, center Harold Mauro once wrestled a monkey at the Jackson County Fair. Kevin Duffy, Brown Marks, and Jim Sniadecki were Star Trek fans. Butcher had to have two hot dogs and a Coke at halftime every game. Terry Cole poured champagne into his Los Angeles hotel bathtub during the Rose Bowl trip.

And then there was the daring John Isenbarger, whose running back nature sometimes kicked in when he was supposed to punt, thus generating the famous "Punt John Punt" chant.

So there you go.

"We had a lot of fun on that team," Stolberg said.

Stolberg's fun came with a shoulder harness to protect his dislocated left shoulder. It prevented him from overextending his arm. It did not prevent him from making a difference.

⋅⟶⟞⟨⟶⋅

The season that no one expected radiated expectation.

Yes, IU had gone 2–8 and 1–8–1 in Pont's first two seasons, but he had recruited well. Talent was there in his third season, a combination of youth and experience.

In fact, Stolberg, Doug Crusan, John Isenbarger, Jade Butcher, Terry Cole, Brown Marks, Cal Snowden, Jim Sniadecki, and Bob Kirk all were either drafted or made an NFL team. Crusan became an All-Pro player. He and Cole played on the Miami Dolphins' unbeaten 1972 Super Bowl championship squad.

Veterans such as Mauro, right guard Bob Russell, Kaczmarek, and fellow linebacker Kevin Duffy provided key leadership.

The Hoosiers, Kaczmarek said, had potential. All they had to do was learn how to win, and if it so often came in nail-biter fashion, no one complained.

Not after the previous two seasons.

"My sophomore and junior years ate at [Pont]," Kaczmarek said. "My sophomore year, I lost the game at Ohio State. It was my fault. I wasn't covering the receivers correctly. I was always in the wrong place at the wrong time.

"Coach Pont was fuming at me. I deserved it."

It was a different era, and coaches sometimes made their point with more than just strong words. Pont was especially upset because he had played for Ohio State coach Woody Hayes and wanted to beat his former coach as a measuring stick on how far he had come.

"If that scene happened today, they'd put him on probation for a week," Kaczmarek said. "I lost the game for him. I understand. You want to beat your mentor. I learned a lot from it."

He paused and smiled.

"I learned to keep my helmet on."

Pont unleashed an offense called the "speed option," which allowed the Hoosiers to—yes—use their speed to blow past defenders. They'd line up in the I-formation, where the quarterback, fullback, and tailback were right behind each other.

In most offenses, this was a power running approach that basically attacked by going straight ahead. In Pont's offense, it was about getting to the perimeter as much as attacking the middle, but you needed the speed to do it. IU had it, more than it had ever had before.

Quarterback Harry Gonso was ridiculously versatile. He was a state diving champ out of Findlay High School in Ohio. He could run the 100-yard dash in 10.2 seconds and was a good enough baseball player for the Detroit Tigers to offer him $15,000 to sign out of high school. Fortunately for the Hoosiers, he turned them down.

Isenbarger was such a good basketball player at Muncie Central High School in Indiana that Kentucky coach Adolph Rupp recruited him. Isenbarger also placed fourth in the state pole vault. Michigan wanted him badly enough that a couple of superstars from its tradition-rich past—1940 Heisman Trophy winner Tom Harmon and ex-All-America Gerald Ford (who would go on to be president of the United States)—sent letters pushing the benefits of being a Wolverine. Isenbarger stuck with IU.

Butcher was a receiver with a knack for finding the end zone. He scored 30 touchdowns in 30 career games with the Hoosiers. That school career receiving record stood for nearly forty years until James Hardy broke it with 36 in 2007.

Isenbarger had been recruited as a quarterback but was switched to tailback ten days before the season opener. Tailback Terry Cole was moved from tailback to fullback so he could be more of a blocker than a runner.

Sometimes you have to sacrifice for the good of the team.

Pont also changed the defense, going from a 5–3 formation to a 4–4, which meant more linebackers and more speed. He got that idea after visiting Alabama and its coach, Paul "Bear" Bryant, who favored a 4–4 scheme. In addition, Pont mandated that players lose weight to improve their speed. For instance, talented offensive lineman Doug Crusan, who would go on to play in the NFL, was switched to defensive tackle and told to lose thirty pounds over the summer to get to 232.

He did.

The result: IU was swift and fit on both sides of the ball.

Beyond that, Kaczmarek said, "The biggest difference was we were all good physically. It was the mental part, studying the game, understanding what offenses can do in certain formations. When you know what you're looking for, when you envision it, as soon as the play starts, you start reacting. You can't wait. It's too late. The game is too fast. The mental aspect is the difference."

That difference showed up right away. The Hoosiers opened by beating Kentucky 12–10, then Kansas 18–15, then Illinois 20–7. Next was a rugged Iowa team, and the Hoosiers were on the verge of defeat.

And then . . .

"There's less than a minute to go," Stolberg said. "We're down 17–14. We call a fake field goal on the 20-yard line. A field goal would have tied the game. We said, 'No, we're going to win.' We called a fake and ran it to the 3-yard line. Next play we scored and won it 21–17. That's the way it was.

"After that game, it was, 'Wow, this is serious.'"

Next came a 27–20 win at Michigan. The unbeaten Hoosiers then headed to Arizona and won 42–7.

"The only team we beat soundly was Arizona out there," Stolberg said. "There was a lot of talk on the West Coast that we would lose badly, and we trounced them. It was a lot of fun."

Fun continued with a 14–9 win against Wisconsin and the victory at Michigan State.

The Hoosiers rolled into their game at Minnesota positioned to win the Big Ten and get to the Rose Bowl. But they lost 33–7 (the Gophers scored 20 fourth-quarter points), which meant everything would be decided by the regular season finale against third-ranked Purdue.

IU won 19–14, and, as usual, it came down to the end.

Purdue was set to take a late lead, getting first and goal at the Hoosier 3-yard line. Fullback Perry Williams tried to blast into the end zone, got blasted by Kaczmarek, and fumbled. IU safety Mike Baughman recovered at the 2-yard line.

Cole played a huge role by punishing a Boiler defense prepared to shut down the perimeter. Cole attacked them up the middle for a series of big plays. He ran for 155 yards and scored the winning touchdown on a 63-yard run.

That gave the Hoosiers a 6–1 Big Ten record, the same as Purdue and Minnesota.

"What's interesting is that if you take all our scores and average them that season," Stolberg said, "we win 19–14. That's the exact score of the Purdue game that put us in the Rose Bowl."

So who would get the Rose Bowl berth?

Purdue had gone the season before. Minnesota had gone a couple of years before that. IU had never gone.

The Big Ten made it clear—the Hoosiers would go to Pasadena.

"We didn't get the word till that night," Stolberg said, "but I didn't have any doubt."

Added Kaczmarek, "We went as champions. That was important."

Indiana would head west to face USC and superstar tailback O.J. Simpson. It would be the Hoosiers' first-ever bowl game, and the cream 'n' crimson faithful were pumped. For Kaczmarek, it was more like, "It's about time. I thought I would play in the Rose Bowl my junior year," he said with a laugh while thinking about that 1–8–1 record. "It didn't quite work out."

What was playing in the Rose Bowl like?

"It was very cool," Stolberg said. "When I ran on the field for the first time, my heart was racing. There were 105,000 fans in the stands. In the stadium, one of the end zones was painted Indiana. There was a big rose in the center of the field. I was so excited."

He wasn't alone in his excitement.

"Playing in the Rose Bowl was why I came to the Big Ten," Kaczmarek said. "That was my dream.

"I could have gone to other Big Ten schools. It was the combination of IU's business school and playing in the Big Ten that intrigued me.

"Being there was unique. I remember seeing all the red. I was shocked at how many people from Indiana came to California. We were treated so well.

"Indiana did a first-class job. It was a beautiful hotel, wonderful meals. A lot of times we practiced double sessions. Just the beauty of the Rose Bowl, practicing for two weeks looking at the mountains; going to Disneyland and all the other attractions was just fantastic."

Then came the game. Top-ranked USC was loaded with stars that included nine eventual NFL first-round draft picks. Simpson was the biggest, but the Trojans also had offensive lineman Ron Yary, the Outland Trophy winner. That award goes to the nation's best lineman.

Coached by John McKay, USC came in with a 9–1 record. They had outscored opponents 258–87. Simpson had rushed for more than 1,400 yards with 11 touchdowns. Quarterback Steve Sogge, directing a run-heavy attack, had thrown for more than 1,000 yards.

Stopping Simpson was the key. The junior had world-class speed; he was a member of the USC NCAA–title-winning 440-yard relay that set a world record in 1967. He'd finished second in voting for the Heisman Trophy, awarded annually to the nation's best player. Simpson would win the award the next season.

To win, IU had to slow Simpson down.

"He was very quick and fast," Kaczmarek said. "Here's what we did. We knew they ran a lot of isolation plays where they ran the fullback. The coaches told us we had to hit these guys straight up. If we took a shoulder, Simpson was going to go the other way. We blitzed them. We were quicker than they were, but they were faster than we were.

"We attacked them and didn't give him a lot of running room. When he did get out, he was tough to bring down."

Simpson got out enough to rush for 128 yards on 25 carries and score 2 touchdowns. Still, USC scored just 14 points.

The Hoosiers scored only 3 points, on David Kornowa's 27-yard second-quarter field goal. IU managed just 189 total yards. Gonso was 9 for 25 for 110 yards and an interception. Isenbarger ran for 38 yards on 12 carries. It wasn't enough.

If a fairy tale season didn't have a fairy tale ending, well, that wasn't the point. Lasting memories were.

"We know we're getting up in age, and with each passing year there will be fewer and fewer of us," Kaczmarek said. "We know our timeline is getting shorter, so we'll try to make the best of all the times we can get together."

Or, as Harold Mauro put it, "When we see each other at our reunions, we don't even shake hands. We hug each other. It's all hugs. That's our handshake."

## CHAPTER 13

# Players Matter

RICHARD LAGOW PERSEVERED.

Did you expect anything less?

Simmie Cobbs overcame.

Was there any doubt?

Tegray Scales thrived.

How could he not?

These are among the difference-making players who contributed so much to the 2017 season and who helped set the foundation for future success.

Programs are built with good people, quality people, people who sweat and bleed for the cause because that's the only way they know how to do it. Tom Allen put together a group of such people, from assistant coaches to staff members to, of course, players.

Here's a look at some of them.

⋆⇒◉ ◉⇐⋆

Lagow had prepared for a breakthrough senior season, doing all that was expected—and more—to help lead the Hoosiers to victory. That included working as a counselor at the annual Manning Passing Academy that summer, where he got pointers from NFL quarterback superstars Peyton and Eli Manning.

The change was noticeable during August camp, says receiver Nick Westbrook. "His confidence is through the roof. He's approaching every day like he's the [starter]. He knows exactly what he's doing. He's holding everybody accountable and making sure everyone is [focused] because we can't have anybody slacking."

Lagow spent plenty of extra time working with offensive co-ordinator Mike DeBord and quarterbacks coach Nick Sheridan, who had been hired the previous winter. They watched films and went over which plays best suited Lagow's style. Beyond that, they strengthened their understanding of each other, something DeBord started in the late 1990s at Michigan while coaching Brian Griese and Tom Brady.

"I've always tried to have a great relationship with the quarter-backs," DeBord says. "I don't get after the quarterback very much. I want him to feel comfortable. I know how hard that position is to play. If I have to say something to him, I'll say it to him in a quiet way.

"A lot of times when everybody watches the game, they're watching the quarterback. All eyes are on that guy. So they feel they're part of the offense as far as the scheme.

"Nick and I talk to Rich and tell him he doesn't have to make plays. Whatever is given, take it. Check it down. You don't have to be a hero. Just be a quarterback. Play the game."

And yet, change was coming.

Backup quarterback Peyton Ramsey, a redshirt freshman, had dual-threat run-and-pass ability that Lagow lacked. That was important because Allen and DeBord wanted an offense that included a running quarterback to put extra stress on the defense.

So Ramsey would see action to start the season—and not just in a mop-up role. IU coaches wanted to see if Ramsey, who had performed well the previous fall on the scout team and then again in spring practice, could thrive under real-game pressure and conditions.

As it turned out, he could.

Still, the starting job was Lagow's to lose. Everyone understood that. He had started all of the previous season as a junior college transfer and led IU to the Foster Farms Bowl game. He'd thrown for 3,362 yards, second most in the Big Ten. He had 21 touchdown passes, which was fine. He had 17 interceptions, which was not so fine.

He had to clean that up, and he knew it.

Lagow came out firing strikes in the season opener against Ohio State. He made big play after big play, totaling 410 passing yards and 3 touchdowns. Yes, he threw 2 interceptions, but one came off a tipped pass, and the other came late while trying to make a play to rally the Hoosiers back.

He became the first IU quarterback with two 400-yard passing games. He set a school record with 65 pass attempts. His job seemed secure.

It was not.

In the next three games, Lagow went 18 for 38 for 251 yards, 1 touchdown, and 1 interception. The 47.4 percent completion percentage wasn't nearly good enough.

The Penn State game was decisive. Lagow struggled with his accuracy in the first half, although he did throw a touchdown pass.

Ramsey played the entire second half against Penn State and couldn't get the Hoosiers in the end zone. He was just 4 for 13 in the final two quarters. Still, his dual-threat ability was enough to convince Hoosier coaches it was time for a change.

For the next three games, Lagow didn't see the field. Behind the scenes, he continued to work. He stayed committed to the cause rather than slide into negativity. He was tougher than that, and there was a reason for that.

Call it the photo in the locker.

The photo was taped to the back wall of Lagow's locker. It showed the uncompromising face of beauty, stripped of pretension and illusion, raw because that's what truth often is. It was the face of the ultimate fighter staring down the ultimate fight—bald head, black smeared under both eyes, raised fists covered by boxing gloves, a smile rather than a snarl because this fight can't be won by nastiness but by faith.

Kara O'Neal sent Lagow her photo because that's what friends do when sharing what matters most. Life isn't all sunshine and rainbows. Adversity stinks, but it so often reveals. O'Neal's adversity came in the form of acute myeloid leukemia, but just call it what it is: cancer.

In retrospect, losing a starting job didn't seem so bad.

"I see her every day," Lagow says. "I have a picture of her in my locker. It keeps me motivated."

"When things aren't going my way," he adds, "when times are tough, you keep your life in perspective. No matter what the situation is, you could be battling cancer. There's always someone who has it worse. Her ability to stay positive and continue fighting is constant motivation for me."

O'Neal and Lagow had been friends since high school in Plano, Texas. He was the hotshot quarterback. She was dating a receiver. They quickly developed a bond.

"It's very important to me," Lagow says of their friendship. "I think it's important to her also. She texted me a couple of days ago. She was thinking about her journey and how much it's helped her, the relationship we have. I see it the same way. I really value our friendship. She can motivate me always, even if we haven't talked for a couple of days."

O'Neal had battled cancer since she was sixteen. First it was oral chemotherapy. Later it became surgery. A full head of hair was a temporary casualty.

Through it all, she didn't quit.

"She and I are strong in our faith," Lagow says. "Having that bond has strengthened it."

The previous season, Lagow had helped lead IU to a 6–6 record and a Fosters Farms Bowl bid against No. 19 Utah in Santa Clara, California. O'Neal watched the Hoosiers lose a heartbreaker from a Dallas hospital bed. Lagow surprised her by writing her name on the towel that always hangs from his belt during games. He took a photo of it and sent it to her before the game.

"I was in the locker room before the game, thinking the season was coming to the end," Lagow says. "We still had a game, of course.

I was trying to process the whole season. Coming from junior college and getting through the whole season, now you're in the 49ers' stadium [Levi's Stadium] playing in a bowl game. I was just enjoying the moment.

"In doing so, I thought about her. I thought I would show my appreciation toward her and our friendship by doing that. It's something I continue to do, put her name on my tape every game."

O'Neal responded by sending Lagow an inspirational message. He later sent her a football signed by all his teammates. She tweeted her thanks: "Received the best gift today. Thank you @RichardLagow and the rest of @HoosierFootball team for making me feel so loved #nevergiveup #fcancer."

A second-half leg injury to Ramsey against Maryland in late October forced Lagow into action. He threw for 131 yards and 2 touchdowns and nearly led the Hoosiers to victory.

That leg injury lingered. Ramsey wasn't able to play. Lagow started the final three games of the season. It was, perhaps, the best stretch of his IU career, and it produced victories over Illinois and Rutgers.

Lagow wound up completing 58.3 percent of his passes for 1,936 yards, 15 touchdowns, and 8 interceptions. Ramsey completed 65.4 percent of his passes for 1,250 yards, 10 touchdowns, and 5 interceptions. He also rushed for 226 yards and 2 TDs.

Through it all, Lagow says, O'Neal helped him persevere.

"Every day I still look at the picture of her in my locker. It puts me in a better mood. It gets my mind right to do what we have to do that day. You put the team above everything else. That's what matters the most. She helps me keep that in perspective.

"How you handle adversity says a lot about yourself. Of course, that's one thing that [NFL officials] can see that. What's bigger than that is my teammates seeing that. My coaches seeing that.

"I want what's best for the team. I'll do anything to help the team and be supportive. If in doing that, the next level notices, 'Hey, Rich has a great attitude, and he's handling it the right way,' that's great."

Adds coach Tom Allen, "It's being a great teammate, cheering [the other player] on, not going over and feeling sorry for yourself when you're not in the game.

"When [the other player] comes off, you're helping him, coaching him, encouraging him, talking about the things he's seeing. You guys have trained all week to prepare to play. Let's work together."

And so Lagow did.

⊷⟳⟲⊷

Simmie Cobbs overcame the death of his father when he was nine years old.

They were as close as a son and father could be. In many ways, they still are. On the left side of Cobbs's chest is a tattoo. It depicts a basketball with wings, adorned by a crown, and supported underneath with the words "Simmie Sr."

"Every time I step on the football field or when I'm alone, I always send him a prayer and talk to him," Cobbs says. "I feel that since I put him on my heart, whenever my chest is beating, he'll still be beating through me, as well."

After his father's death, Cobbs lived with his grandmother, great aunt, an uncle, and a couple of cousins on the west side of Chicago. It wasn't the safest part of town, and Cobbs sometimes slept at a friend's house or stayed with neighbors.

Eventually, a friend, Robert Spillane, invited Cobbs to stay with his family in Oak Park, Illinois. Cobbs was entering his sophomore year of high school. Spillane's parents, Gretchen and Michael, were all for it.

The arrangement included a strong dose of football. Gretchen's father was Johnny Lattner, the 1953 Heisman Trophy winner from Notre Dame. Robert went on to play linebacker at Western Michigan.

At IU, Cobbs saw limited action as a freshman then had a breakthrough sophomore season, catching 60 passes for 1,035 yards and

4 touchdowns. He only played 1 snap in the 2016 season after breaking his leg in the season opener.

He came back to have a monster season in 2017, starting from the opener against Ohio State, when he had 11 catches for 149 yards. At six-foot-four and 220 pounds, Cobbs was big enough, fast enough, and athletic enough to dominate anyone who tried to cover him.

He finished with 72 catches for 841 yards and 8 touchdowns.

"He's that rock there that you can count on," Tom Allen says.

⊷⊜ ⊜⊷

History will rate Tegray Scales as one of the greatest linebackers Indiana has ever had, on par with previous Hoosier All-Americans Ken Kaczmarek and Joe Norman. Scales's success, teammate Tony Fields says came because, "He's accountable. You can always count on him, whether it's a game or a workout or being a teammate. Anything he does, he's focused on the details. That causes you to focus on your details. Trust is the biggest thing with him."

Scales's efficiency caught Allen's eye.

"He's quick and athletic, but he isn't necessarily a burner," Allen says. "He's not an exceptionally fast guy. So how is he effective? There's no wasted motion. His footwork is clean. He doesn't take false steps.

"He's flourished in the system we have. His skill set fits it. We read the backfield, and he's really good at it. He's able to anticipate."

Scales thrived without ego.

"Most of the plays I do make, I'm supposed to make," he says. "So it's not like, 'Oh, good job.' It's what I'm supposed to do. Coach puts me in position to make those plays. My job is to make them. I did what I'm supposed to."

Who knows what Scales could have accomplished if he had wrestled as well as played football at IU? As a high school senior wrestler at Cincinnati Colerain, he was ranked No. 13 nationally at 195 pounds (he had a career prep record of 154–29) but decided to focus on football in college.

"I love football. I would have wrestled in college if they had a weight class between 197 and heavyweight.

"I'm 225. I'm not wrestling heavyweight. If they had a 230- or 225-pound class, I'd do it. That gap is too big for me. I'm not dropping to 197 and I don't feel like wrestling 285."

That wrestling background had Scales contemplating a shot at MMA, mixed martial arts, which is a combination of boxing and wrestling.

"I'm good at preparing myself for what the future holds. I know it will come to an end. You won't ever see me down. Take one day at a time; live for today."

⋆⇁⊜ ⊜⇂⋆

No one in Indiana football history ever had a knack for breaking up passes like cornerback Rashard Fant. He did it 53 times in a career that started when he was basically 160 pounds, so small you wondered if he would break trying to tackle Big Ten running backs and receivers.

Fant grew to 180 pounds as a senior, delivering big-time impact rather than big-time size. In 49 career games, he set records for passes defended (58) as well as pass breakups. He totaled 132 tackles with 5 interceptions (1 pick-six) and 3 fumble recoveries.

As a junior, he ranked second nationally with 17 pass breakups and third nationally with 20 passes defended. As a senior, he made All-Big Ten second team. He had 24 tackles, broke up 9 passes, and had 1 interception and 1 fumble recovery.

Then there was kicker Griffin Oakes, who delivered as remarkable a turnaround as you're likely to see en route to winning first-team All-Big Ten honors and his second Big Ten kicker-of-the-year award.

Oakes was 16 for 17 on field goals and 38 for 39 on extra points—and technically didn't miss either of those. Both kicks were blocked. He made his final 11 field goals of the season.

Beyond that, Oakes led the Big Ten and was second nationally in field goal percentage (94.1). He was 15 for 15 from inside the 50-yard line, including 4 of 4 from 40–49 yards. He was one of eight kickers nationally with at least one 50-yarder and an 85.0 percent or better accuracy.

The result: Oakes made first-team All-Big Ten after a disappointing junior season, in which he was just 16 for 26 on field goals.

In 2015, as a sophomore, he was Big Ten kicker of the year after making 24 of 29 field goals.

Oakes set a school career record with 69 field goals. He's second with 147 extra points and 354 total points. He joined Scott Bonnell as the only IU kickers to twice earn first-team all-conference honors.

Also making first-team All-Big Ten was Scales. That followed a junior season in which he earned SI.com All-America honors. Before Scales, the Hoosiers hadn't had a first-team linebacker since Joe Huff and Willie Bates in 1988. Scales led IU with 12.5 tackles for loss and 2 interceptions. He added 6 sacks and 2 fumble recoveries plus 89 tackles. For his career, Scales's 46 tackles for loss were third in program history. He was tenth with 325 total tackles. He had 13 double-digit tackle games.

Also making first-team All-Big Ten on offense was Cobbs. He was second in the Big Ten in receptions (72), third in yardage (841), and fourth in receiving touchdowns (8). He had three 100-yard receiving games.

Also, six Hoosiers earned defensive or special teams honorable mention all-conference notice: senior linebacker Chris Covington, junior safety Jonathan Crawford, senior safety Chase Dutra, junior return specialist J-Shun Harris, senior defensive end Robert Mc-Cray III, and sophomore punter Haydon Whitehead.

Three offensive players received honorable mention: senior tight end Ian Thomas, junior left guard Wes Martin, and junior receiver Luke Timian.

That gave IU a school-record thirteen players honored by the Big Ten. The previous record in a year was twelve in 2015 and 2016.

At the season-ending team banquet, Scales won the Anthony Thompson Most Valuable Player Award. Lagow won the inaugural LEO (Love Each Other) Award created by Allen.

Scales was the first player to win consecutive team MVP honors since Jammie Kirlew in 2008 and '09.

Here were the other team award winners from the 2017 banquet:

Offensive Newcomer of the Year: Morgan Ellison
Defensive Newcomer of the Year: Raheem Layne
Ted Whereatt Senior Academic Excellence Award: Rashard Fant
Ted Verlihay Mental Attitude Award: Danny Friend
Corby Davis Memorial Award (Outstanding Back): Ricky Brookins
Howard Brown Dedication to IU Football Award: Nate Hoff
Chris Dal Sasso Award (Outstanding Lineman): Greg Gooch, Wes Martin
Harold Mauro Loyalty to IU Football Award: Tony Fields
Terry P. Cole Award (Old Oaken Bucket Game MVP): Chase Dutra, Griffin Oakes
Offensive Scout Team Players of the Year: Alex Rodriguez, Nick Tronti
Defensive Scout Team Player of the Year: Joshua Brown
Outstanding Walk-On Player of the Year: Ben Bach
Special Teams Player of the Year: Chase Dutra
Most Outstanding Specialist of the Year: Griffin Oakes
Offensive Player of the Year: Simmie Cobbs Jr.
Defensive Player of the Year: Chris Covington
Anthony Thompson Most Valuable Player: Tegray Scales
Team Captains: Greg Gooch, Richard Lagow, Wes Martin, Tegray Scales
LEO Award: Richard Lagow

Finally, no Hoosier summed up the cream 'n' crimson experience better than Fant with his end-of-season open letter to fans:

A Note to Indiana University from Rashard Fant

*Dear Indiana University,*

THANK YOU! I feel it is only appropriate to begin this letter with those two words because of everything that you have given me, shown me, and experienced with me. I came to Bloomington as an 18 year-old boy, but now I am leaving here as a soon to be (January 8th) 23 year-old man! I must admit that prior to arriving on campus, I did not know much about this prestigious university other than it was known for basketball and being the birthplace of Kappa Alpha Psi Fraternity. Honestly, when I first received an offer from IU, attending here was the last thing on my mind. Without hesitation, I can say that I am so thankful I ultimately chose to come to IU! I have met many amazing people during my time here, have had life changing experiences and conversations, and have had the opportunity to get out of my comfort zone and find myself as a person. It was not always easy during my time here, but each time I had to face and overcome adversity, it helped me grow as a student, as a football player, and most importantly as a man. As a student, IU has given me more than I could have ever asked for . . . a Bachelor's degree, soon to be a Master's degree, department and community engagement and outreach experiences, all while playing the game that I love.

I came to IU thinking that I might be able to continue what I had started in high school, which was to help build up and contribute to a football program. I wanted to help bring more of a winning mindset to this football team. However, what I was actually given was the opportunity to accomplish more than I could have imagined both on the field and within the community. Although we did not win a B1G or a national championship, we got to the first bowl game in eight years, then made it back-to-back bowl games the next year, all while beating Purdue four times in a row, and being able to improve the defense to one of the best IU has seen in years. I think that could definitely be considered helping to turn a program around and working toward holding each other and the program to a higher standard. With that being said, as I leave, I hope that I am not remembered as an All-Big Ten cornerback or any other statistic or catchphrase, but rather as a great representative of all that this university and athletic department hopes to instill during a student's time here. I always talk about how my goal in life is to positively affect as many lives as possible. Being a student-athlete at Indiana University gave me unlimited opportunities to do just that. I only hope that, whether it was a brief encounter or a lifelong friendship, anyone whose path I crossed would say that the thing they appreciated about me the most was that I cared about people, was positive, and wanted to bring laughter and smiles to the faces of people, whether I knew them or not.

Coach Shelby and I always talk about leaving a place better than it was when you arrived, and I believe I have done that and hope those who know me would agree. Lastly, I want to say thank you to the administration at IU who helped me grow as a man and provided me with everything I needed in order to succeed at IU, giving me opportunities that allowed me to reach far beyond the sidelines to make a difference in both the community and the department. Thank you to Coach Shelby, the many teammates and coaches I have had over the last four-and-a-half years that believed in me, have helped me grow as a player, and have aided in my success on the field. Thank you to all of the professors that have worked with me, challenged me, and that have taken the time to not only educate me but to get to know me as a person. I want to give a special thank you to Professor Cheryl Hughes for impacting my life in the greatest way a professor ever has! Thank you to the fans who have not only cheered the team on but also believed in me every step of the way. We know it was not always easy and there was a LOT of heartbreak, but my teammates and I definitely appreciate you all sticking with us. While I cannot say that I was in a rush to do so, I am now excited to be a part of the loyal fan base of the IU Football team and I cannot wait to see the Breakthrough that will come soon. Last but not least . . . I want to say, thank you to the "24 Sports 1 Team" Family! As athletes, we share many characteristics although we play different sports, but the support we provide for each other is second to none. I came here thinking "24 Sports 1 Team" was just some catchy mantra on the walls, but actually it is what the athletic programs here truly live by and I am honored and proud to have been a part of it. Bloomington is not just some city in Indiana or where my school is located, it is a part of me for life. It is my second home!

For the athletes that will come after me here at IU, and especially in the football program, remember these three things:

1. Your sport is not who you are; it is what you do. Find yourself outside of athletics!
2. You are a part of something that is bigger than yourself!
3. Leave a place or a team better than it was when you joined it!

Much Love,
Rashard Fant #16

"Be strong and courageous. Do not be afraid or terrified because of them, for the Lord your God goes with you; he will never leave you nor forsake you." —*Deuteronomy 31:6*

# Coaches and Staff Matter

A HEAD COACH IS ONLY AS GOOD AS THE PEOPLE AROUND him or her, and Tom Allen assembled a group of coaches and staff members to fit his passionate, caring style.

Here's a look at those who contributed to the 2017 season, and beyond.

⋯⋙◉⋘⋯

Mike DeBord, offensive coordinator, was top priority after Allen was hired as head coach. He needed to find someone to run the offense. Allen had the defensive covered (he retained his role as defensive coordinator), but he wanted an experienced coach who could deliver a versatile attack that varied tempo (sometimes snapping the ball in less than fifteen seconds, sometimes using most of the play clock), used multiple weapons, and capitalized on quarterback runs.

As Allen put it, he wanted someone to be the "head coach of the offense."

Enter DeBord, who left Tennessee to return to his Indiana roots. He grew up in Muncie and played football at Manchester College near Fort Wayne. His brother Eric played for the Hoosiers and coach Lee Corso.

Back in the late 1970s, DeBord had visited with Allen's father, Tom Sr., a successful high school coach, to learn how to run the split-back veer attack. While at Michigan in the late 1990s, DeBord got to know Allen better while DeBord recruited Ben Davis athletes.

DeBord coached at Michigan a couple of different times and was the offensive coordinator when the Wolverines won the 1997 national championship. He also coached at Northwestern and in the NFL and was the head coach for four years at Central Michigan. In 2016, in DeBord's last season at Tennessee, the Volunteers averaged 36.4 points and 443.7 yards a game.

In his first season at IU, DeBord directed an attack that averaged 26.8 points and 395.8 yards.

⊷⇒◎⇐⊶

Mark Hagen, defensive line coach, was a former All-Big Ten linebacker at IU. He previously coached at Northern Illinois, Purdue, and Texas A&M.

⊷⇒◎⇐⊶

Mike Hart, running backs coach, is Michigan's all-time leading rusher with 5,040 yards. He played three years for the Indianapolis Colts, and previously coached at Eastern Michigan, Western Michigan, and Syracuse.

⊷⇒◎⇐⊶

Grant Heard, wide receivers coach, was a receiver at Mississippi and then for the San Francisco 49ers and the Pittsburgh Steelers. He previously coached at North Carolina State, Mississippi, Western Michigan, Lambuth, and Arkansas State.

⊷⇒◎⇐⊶

Darren Hiller, offensive line coach, played offensive line for West Texas A&M. He previously coached at Arkansas–Monticello, Northwestern State, Arkansas State, Nevada, Cincinnati, and South Florida.

⊷⇒◎⇐⊶

William Inge, linebackers coach, earned All-Big Ten honorable mention recognition while playing at Iowa. He previously coached at Iowa, Northern Iowa, Colorado, San Diego State, Cincinnati, Buffalo, and the NFL's Buffalo Bills.

⋗═◎═◁

Noah Joseph, safeties coach, made his mark as a defensive back at Drake, where he set the school record with a 100-yard interception return for a touchdown. He previously coached at Drake, Eastern Kentucky, Iowa State, Eastern Illinois, Montana State, and North Texas.

⋗═◎═◁

Brandon Shelby, cornerbacks coach, was an All-Big Twelve defensive back at Oklahoma. He previously coached at Oklahoma, Arizona, San Diego, Portland State, and Louisiana-Monroe.

⋗═◎═◁

Nick Sheridan, quarterbacks coach, started four games as quarterback at Michigan. He previously coached at Western Kentucky, South Florida, and Tennessee.

⋗═◎═◁

Keith Caton, strength and conditioning coach, played at Southern Mississippi. He previously worked at Southern Mississippi, Auburn, Elon, Western Kentucky, Missouri, and Baylor.

⋗═◎═◁

Mike Doig, director of football operations, is a former high school football and basketball coach and high school athletic director. He

led Grace Christian Academy to the Tennessee state basketball
semifinals from 2015–17.

-+⇒◎⊜+-

Mike Pechac, director of player development and academic en-
hancement, previously coached at Malone College and Hiram College. He also worked at Ohio State, Otterbein College, and Bowling
Green.

-+⇒◎⊜+-

Mark Deal, assistant athletic director for Alumni relations, works
closely with football. A former IU player and assistant coach, his
passion for all things cream 'n crimson runs deep. His father, Russ,
played on the Hoosiers' 1945 Big Ten title team. Older brother Mike
played on the 1967 Rose Bowl team. His daughter, Carrie, played
volleyball at IU and earned academic All-Big Ten honors.

-+⇒◎⊜+-

Kate Miller, assistant director of operations/senior staff assistant,
plays a huge role in organizing and providing behind-the-scenes
guidance and support. A former University of Idaho swimmer, she
ensures things run smoothly in the office and on road trips.

-+⇒◎⊜+-

Jeff Keag, senior assistant athletic director, is in charge of all media
relations, interview requests and more. He ensures everything runs
smoothly and efficiently from a public relations standpoint. He's
instrumental in getting out information, organizing Tom Allen's
media obligations, and promoting all aspects of the program.

-+⇒◎⊜+-

Greg Kincaid, assistant director, provides invaluable assistance in media relations, information release, interviews, and more.

The strength staff consists of Matt Clapp, Paul Constantine, Rick Danison, and Jon Fleury

The support staff consists of Billy Cosh (offense), Pat Kuntz (defense), John Morookian (offense), Jim Nelson (defense), Jeff McInerney (special teams), Ryan McInerney (defense), Sean Fisher (offense), Matt Wilson (director of recruiting), Scott Gasper (director of player personnel), Kasey Teegardin (director of on-campus recruiting), Mitch Gudmundson (director of football equipment), Carter Uebelhoer (football equipment manager), Joe Baron (football video coordinator), Jayse McQuaig (assistant football video coordinator), Jay Lotter (digital media designer), Kelsey Zamore (staff assistant), Danielle Mach (sports performance dietitian), Josh Tasma (research assistant/assistant athletic trainer)

The medical staff is overseen by Anthony Thompson (senior associate athletic director) and consists of Kyle Blackmon (head football athletic trainer), Collin Francis (assistant football athletic trainer), Jon Wicks (assistant football athletic trainer), Chelsea Best (assistant football athletic trainer), Andy Hipskind (senior assistant athletic director), Peter Maiers (orthopedic surgeon), and Terry Horner (neurosurgeon).

The entire group is crucial to Indiana success on and off the field. When problems arise, they are at the forefront in fixing them. They are a dedicated group of men and women who help ensure Hoosier players have all the necessary resources and support for success on the field, in the classroom, and in life.

## CHAPTER 15

# And So It Begins

A NEW INDIANA FOOTBALL ERA BEGAN AMID CRISP sunshine, high energy, a bullhorn, and a recruiting commitment from the state's top-rated athlete.

In other words, it was a heckuva day.

Tom Allen paced the practice fields on the first day of August 2017 camp, focused, passionate, and ready for another debut as a college head football coach to follow efforts in spring practice and the annual Big Ten media gathering in Chicago.

"Be finishers, guys!" he shouted, a theme he'd pushed since he got the job nine months earlier.

The biggest debut of all loomed in four weeks—the season opener against perennial powerhouse Ohio State, a home game Allen called the "biggest in school history"—and plenty of work needed to be done.

Allen armed himself with coaching essentials—lemon drops to soothe overworked vocal cords, a bullhorn to limit the stress on those vocal cords and ensure he would be heard, a hat and sunglasses to shield out the sun, and a tolerance for music nearly every coach in America would rather skip. Officially, it's called trap music, which is part hip hop, part dance music, part repetitiveness, and all courtesy of IU's strength coaches and young male preference.

And so 21 Savage rapped the song "Numb" from practice field loudspeakers, then followed minutes later with "Bank Account." It was loud, and it was not Sinatra. Then came Kodak Black's "First Day Out," which seemed appropriate for the first day of training camp until you realized Kodak Black was trapping about his first day out of jail. No matter. It fit the high-energy mood crucial to high-level preparation necessary for the breakthrough season Allen pushed.

Practices were divided into five-minute segments, with each segment addressing different areas, a mix of fundamental work, drills, and plays. Quarterbacks drilled throwing to receivers without any defensive backs covering them. A few minutes later, defensive backs arrived. Then it became eleven offensive players against eleven defensive players. Short-pass accuracy didn't translate to deep balls, which was what you'd expect on the first day.

Returning starting quarterback Richard Lagow led the way, which was also what you'd expect, with redshirt freshman Peyton Ramsey and true freshman Nick Tronti right behind him. A veteran cornerback got beat on a deep ball, and it didn't matter that the receiver dropped the ball. Cornerback coach Brandon Shelby instantly addressed it—"Get your eyes up. That's why you got beat."

At one point, defensive line coach Mark Hagen made an emphatic fundamental point: "Head up! You can't see what's going on with your head down."

Through it all, sweat bees did what sweat bees do—buzz and sting. The Hoosiers pushed to sting—and the Buckeyes topped their list.

This was the personification of Allen's first-ever August camp as a college head coach. He'd thought it out well in advance, learning from the men he'd coached under and for the father he'd played for. Shortly after day one was history, he offered perspective.

"You kind of pull from the different coaches you've worked with. Everybody has different strengths and things that you like about how we did things, then maybe things you didn't. I think you culminate all those, bring them together, and try to come up with the best structure in terms of the day.

"One thing I'm real big on is our guys taking care of their bodies throughout fall camp. I'm trying to structure a schedule where we can maximize their rest in terms of our sleep time. There's a lot of studies that show the ability to increase recovery time from injuries and just your ability to compete at a high level, as long as you take advantage of [sleep time].

"That's about being a pro. I say that all the time to our guys. We educate them [in an] extremely detailed [way] about what that means. We want to create a calendar both in the way that our days are structured and the way that our time is structured where we can maximize recovery time. When we're going, we're going full bore. It's very intense and very demanding. Then we've got to get our bodies back.

"At the same time, we're going to have more team meetings at the end. I just like to have everybody together and get into their heads and shape their mind-set. I'm a big believer in that. We won't do it every single night, but we want to build team, mind-set, and culture, the way we want our guys to think, be able to come together. That's a little bit different."

And then, because football is just as much physical as mental, Allen wanted to practice the toughest moments to get the best possible result.

"We do a lot of situational work. We try to create game-like situations to create those breakthrough opportunities we've talked about. We did a study on that all last off-season here, all those opportunities we had in games that were close, be able to recreate those in practice as best we can so we can be able to change the outcome."

The outcome is already changing. A few hours later, Indianapolis Ben Davis's Reese Taylor became IU's fourteenth commitment for the class of 2018. He was a do-it-all high school quarterback who was listed as an athlete with elite ability that included a 4.53 40-yard dash and 38–9 vertical leap. As a senior, he won Indiana's Mr. Football Award while throwing for 3,150 yards and 40 touchdowns and rushing for 802 yards and 15 TDs; as a junior, he threw for nearly 2,800 yards, rushed for nearly a thousand yards, and combined for 34 touchdowns.

It reflected Allen's commitment to winning in-state recruiting battles and landing the talent necessary to beat the Ohio States of the world.

For motivation leading to Ohio State, Allen tried something new: the Scale of Justice. It was a scale placed in the Memorial Stadium team room. Each side of the scale had twenty-five coins to represent the twenty-five practice days before the season opener against Ohio State.

"We have twenty-five opportunities to prepare for Ohio State," Allen said. "On one scale, we have all [Ohio State's] opportunities, and we assume they will take advantage of all theirs. Every day based on how we practice and prepare, we get to add to our side of the scale. We're trying to deposit on that side of the scale. It's a way to visualize that process on a daily basis.

"We want to tip those scales in our favor by August thirty-first."

On the second practice day, the music of choice flashed back to the 1980s AC/DC hit "Hells Bells." Quarterbacks worked on deep balls, with inconsistent success, in part because of windy conditions. Allen continued to use the bullhorn.

Off to the side, cornerbacks did drill work, and Brandon Shelby got into it.

"Let's go! Pick it up!" he shouted.

Meanwhile, receiver Nick Westbrook celebrated a touchdown, and quarterback Richard Lagow ran down the field to chest bump tight end Ian Thomas following a big play.

Then came a day of rest with an overnight trip to nearby Lake Monroe. Players had a 10:00 p.m. curfew. Activities included swimming, putting, cornhole, cards, and volleyball.

Practice resumed the next day, and the quarterbacks looked sharp, but so did the secondary.

"Nice job on coverage," Allen shouted via bullhorn. "Execute. Both sides execute!"

The hurry-up offense showed good energy. A running back busted a big run, which irritated Allen tremendously.

"Are you kidding me?" he shouted.

Defensive linemen drilled hitting sleds and bursting from the snap. Not everyone had the desired burst. Defensive line coach Mark Hagen noticed.

"Get set! Do you want an invitation?" he shouted with a tone that suggested no invitation was coming.

Allen saw a couple of defensive players not make plays.

"That's not good enough," he shouted.

Offensive line coach Darren Hiller educated his guys on pushing the pace before each snap. "Hurry up! What the hell are you waiting on?"

And so it went.

To ensure the Hoosiers were fit enough to handle the upcoming seasons, Allen unleashed strength coach Keith Caton, who stalked the practice fields with enough intensity to scare off a grizzly at twenty yards. On this sun-splashed morning, he wore a sleeveless black shirt and a scowl. A harsh sun glistened off his tanned shaved head. Sunglasses and a goatee added to the intensity. He looked like the baddest dude on the field with bodybuilder biceps and nonstop energy. He was everywhere the players were. The defense forced a fumble, and he thrust an arm out to show the ball was going the other way. The offense made a big play, and he was part of the celebration.

Caton did not coach football. He didn't devise an offense or set a defense. But he was crucial in Allen's raise-the-bar plans. As the head strength and conditioning coach, his job was to ensure the Hoosiers were physically ready for an up-tempo pace and a gauntlet of a schedule.

"We're going to make sure guys can run, that they can go over and over," he said.

Caton prepared for this role after spending four years as Baylor's director of football performance. The Bears were 40–12 during his time there. He'd also worked at Western Kentucky, Missouri, Elon, Auburn, and Southern Mississippi.

But with Allen's breakthrough season goal, the stakes had never been higher. Full pads came out, hitting happened, and more was coming. It was day nine of August's twenty-five-day football immersion, and plenty of work remained.

That said, plenty of work already had been done. Caton had the usual tools of his trade: free weights, machines, sleds, stop watches, and whistles. They have been used, in some manner, for decades. But now there was also new technology such as GPS units and heart-rate monitors. We live in an information age unlike any other. Never before had coaches had so much to work with. The key is making the most of it. Take the GPS devices. Caton used them not to keep a Big Brother eye on players to ensure they weren't breaking curfew but to track yardage and velocity. You could monitor how far players had gone and how fast they were moving.

Add that to heart rate monitors, which show how hard players are working, and you could tailor workouts to maximize training and, hopefully, performance.

"During the summer we do heart-rate things," Caton said. "We put a monitor on guys when they're sprinting or doing sleds. We look at their heart rates and decide from that when we actually need to go again."

The days of having guys run until they throw up were over. Well, mostly.

"The high-tech stuff comes more into effect now because you have guys who weigh 250 to 300 pounds who are fast and explosive," Caton said. "You try to build week by week and not overdo it."

Strength development was big during the summer and remained big in August camp. Caton continued to monitor players to maximize preparation, which was especially huge with the season opener against Ohio State looming in three and a half weeks.

"During practice, one of my guys writes down yardage on players," Caton said. "Coach Allen does a great job of looking at practice and how the guys are moving."

Would the high-tech approach continue during games?

"You can use GPS during games," Caton said. "It's a little harder to do heart-rate monitors during games. All that data you look at afterward. Most people use the GPS stuff during practice, when you can increase or decrease things. On game days, it's too much data when you're trying to run plays and make calls."

Conditioning for football is different than, say, in basketball because of its physical nature. You have to get used to getting hit as well as hitting. There are collisions on every play, and the body has to handle that along with everything else.

"We run the guys all summer and get them in great shape, but you have to put the pads on and get in that football shape," Caton said. "We're going to make sure guys can keep going. That's a big reason why we use the monitors.

"We'll do conditioning, and when a guy's heart rate comes back down, we're hitting another rep at full speed. As the season goes on, they get used to having the pads and banging on each other. We do a lot of running and condition to mimic how the games go."

Allen and offensive coordinator Mike DeBord installed a fast-pace offense that required maximum fitness and strength. At times they hoped to run plays every fifteen seconds or less, although varying the tempo was part of the way to keep defenses off balance. Caton trained the players accordingly.

"You have to manage your volume and your intensities," he said. "We really harp on those guys about recovery."

Meanwhile, the clock ticked toward a nationally televised opener that would, in almost every way, set a tone for the season.

As it turned out, not in the way the Hoosiers had hoped.

CHAPTER 16

# Ohio State

DEFENSIVE COACHES GATHER IN THE WAR ROOM, A LARGE
office in Memorial Stadium's North End Zone facility, to plan for
Ohio State.

Officially, it's known as the Phil Dickens War Room. It's named
after the former IU head coach from 1958 to 1964. It was created
through a donation by the "Dickens boys" (former Hoosier players
under Dickens) and honored the 1958 season, when the Hoosiers
went 5–3–1 and Dickens was named Midwest Coach of the Year.

The white walls are covered in diagrams and code words that
have meaning for those in the know and cause confusion for those
who are not. There are names of cities and terms such as "crank"
and "crash" and "stick." Basically, these are ways the Hoosiers plan
to attack and defend an Ohio State offense that brings both known
and unknown to the challenge.

Former IU head coach Kevin Wilson is the Buckeyes' new offensive coordinator. He is considered one of the most innovative
offensive minds in the country. He will blend his expertise to that
of the high-powered offense run by Ohio State head coach Urban
Meyer. Because this is the season opener, no one in the room knows
what that will look like.

Tom Allen sits at the end of a table. A projector flashes video of
the morning practice. He uses a laser to point to plays made and
not made, correct position achieved and not achieved, of defensive
formations that could be used or not.

"How do you guys feel about this?" he asks.

Then he answers his own question.

"I like cage. I don't like stick. I do like crank. I don't like crash."

He pauses.

"We're setting ourselves up to get what we like on first and second downs."

So now you know.

It's not all business. Safeties coach Noah Joseph mentions that he has bought a TV package for the upcoming Mayweather-McGregor fight and has invited those who are interested to stop by his house. Interest is expressed, and then focus returns to Ohio State.

"We have to bait them into things they don't really want," Allen says.

The video shows an anticipated Ohio State formation and play run by the Hoosier scout team.

"We have to have an answer for this," Allen says. "We've just got to get it figured out."

You can feel the anticipation and focus in the room. These coaches have been preparing for this game for months. Getting powerhouse Ohio State to Memorial Stadium in a Thursday night season opener is generating national attention. That includes ESPN's *College GameDay*, a huge opportunity for IU.

Allen doesn't want to make it bigger than it is, but the stakes are potentially program-changingly huge. The second-ranked Buckeyes are national title contenders. A victory would shock the college football world, generate national acclaim, and potentially jump-start the breakthrough season the Hoosiers are determined to achieve.

The Buckeyes are blessed with superior speed, athleticism, and depth, but Allen has developed his own nationwide reputation as a defensive coach. He was the defensive coordinator under Wilson a year ago. Now he's trying to devise a way to beat whatever Wilson and Ohio State throw at them.

"Schematically, I feel good about this," Allen says.

Will he feel the same after the game?
The clock ticks toward an answer.

⋰⇒○⇐⋰

They came in cars and RVs. They came at eight o'clock in the morning, bearing grills and tents and assorted beverages. They came in crimson, and they came in scarlet, and you couldn't confuse similar colors for similar expectations.

Ohio State arrived with a national title-contending aura and a fan base of epic passion. IU hosted with hope, faith, and a first-time college coach eager to prove he belonged.

Tom Allen did, of course, and if critics wondered why a national search wasn't conducted in the aftermath of former coach Kevin Wilson's departure, they didn't understand the man, and they sure didn't understand his drive.

The first step: shatter that here-we-go-again mentality that comes from generations of losing football.

"A breakthrough is a mind-set," Allen says "It's a culture change. It's an expectation."

As the game approached, buildup escalated.

"The good Lord has a sense of humor when you think about the way this has all played out," Allen says. "To have this as our first game—my first game as head coach, and [Wilson] hired me, and now he's the offensive coordinator there, and I'm the defensive coordinator here. It's an interesting matchup. But once the game starts, it's not about he and I. It's Indiana against Ohio State."

At Ohio State, reporters ask Wilson if Indiana had an edge because their coaches know what he likes to do.

"I'd like to know what I like to do," he says, "because I don't know. I never had a playbook. You go with what works and what the guys are and the way you attack. You have a game plan, and as soon as you get hit in the mouth and things happen, you wad that up. You've got to have the ability to adapt and adjust."

Allen's preparation included watching film of Indiana from recent years with Wilson running the offense.

"This is a very unique situation," Allen says. "I've never been a part of anything like it before. We're also focusing on personnel and scheme that Ohio State has been running. It's a combination of both."

Indiana went big on the pregame buildup, including fireworks, a two-jet flyby, and a national anthem sung by Jim Cornelison, the Chicago Blackhawks' acclaimed singer.

During the traditional pregame walk from Assembly Hall to Memorial Stadium, where coaches and players mingle with fans, Allen got emotional. While wearing a suit, he jumped to give high-fives to cheering IU students.

"I got tears in my eyes," he says. "It was my first walk as head coach. It means so much to me. So many friends and family cheering us on. You have a lot of pride in who you represent. It's personal. It's special."

The Hoosiers won the coin toss and deferred. That meant Ohio State would get the ball first, and the Allen-versus-Wilson drama would begin immediately.

The Buckeyes took a 3–0 lead. Indiana responded with sharp passing by quarterback Richard Lagow. The drive ended with Lagow throwing an 18-yard touchdown pass to Ian Thomas. The Hoosiers ended the first quarter ahead 7–3.

During the break after the first quarter, former IU football coach Lee Corso was honored. He had no problem returning to the school that fired him, unlike another ex-Hoosier coach who, like Voldemort, shall remain nameless.

Ohio State scored 10 second-quarter points. Lagow hit Simmie Cobbs with an 8-yard TD pass. Indiana had a 14–13 halftime lead.

Sold out Memorial Stadium was buzzing.

Still, Allen issued a warning during an ESPN interview: "We're playing our tails off, but we've been here before. There's no moral victories. It's about finishing."

Ohio State took its first lead early in the third quarter on quarterback J. T. Barrett's 2-yard touchdown run. Indiana came right back with its own touchdown, a 2-yard pass from Lagow to Thomas. With five minutes left in the third quarter, the Hoosiers led 21–20. They were twenty minutes away from a stunning upset.

Then the Buckeyes caught fire. They scored the game's final 29 points and won 49–21.

With a basically nonexistent rushing attack (the Hoosiers managed just 17 yards), Lagow took charge. He threw for 410 yards and 3 touchdowns.

Cobbs had 11 catches for 149 yards. Luke Timian had 10 for 72. In all, ten different receivers caught at least 1 pass.

It wasn't enough.

⟜⟶ ⟵⟝

It's about finishing. It's always been about finishing. IU had spent the last couple of years living under a what-if cloud. They played tough but buckled just enough to lose close. They made five plays when six were needed.

Indiana lost their offense in the second half, mostly because Ohio State's attack defense shut down nearly everything. Meanwhile, the Hoosier defense buckled, a victim of the Buckeyes' superior speed and a tactical change that got their really fast guys in space. The defense blinked, in part, because Wilson forced it to. The Hoosiers refused to get beat by the deep vertical pass, so Wilson went with crossing routes that matched his speed guys against IU's.

Twice it turned into a second-half mismatch, with Parris Campbell outracing IU defenders for a 74-yard touchdown. Three minutes later, Ohio State's Johnnie Dixon did the same thing for a 59-yard TD.

"They put us in some conflicts," Allen said after the game. "We had a couple of busts. You make one mistake, and it's a big play. They are so fast, it's hard to catch them."

That bothered Allen because it reflected effort and focus as much as sheer speed. If the Hoosiers had stayed sharp and detailed, they would have prevented the big plays.

"It should have been catches and tackles," Allen said. "That's the part that frustrates me, giving up those kind of plays, because those are avoidable."

Ohio State punished with waves of talent Indiana couldn't match, which didn't surprise. The Buckeyes flourished with four- and five-star recruits at basically every position. The Hoosiers developed with three-star guys.

"We're still not where we need to be depth wise," Allen said. "It is what it is. We have to recruit better so when we take out our number ones, there's not too big of a drop-off. Right now, there is too big of a drop-off."

The day after the game was Friday. It was an off day for players but not coaches. Some assistants would go out recruiting. The rest would search for answers.

But first there was a postgame locker room speech to give. Allen paced in the center of the locker room as the Hoosiers gathered in front of him. A game was lost but not a season. He aimed to deliver perspective, not drama. It wasn't a time to shred but to inspire. A trip to Virginia was next, and one loss couldn't become two. Allen didn't rant or blow up. Contained fury found him in preacher mode in front of a group of kneeling players.

"Field goals weren't going to beat this team," he said. "We were going to be aggressive. We get this flushed. That's all we focus on— is that clear?"

"Yes, sir," the players said.

"For two and a half quarters, we took it to them. We were not able to finish. That's on me. We've got to get key stops. That's on us. If you made a mistake, flush it.

"I'm very disappointed, especially defensively. We have to finish better. We learn from this and move on."

And then Allen pushed perspective and wisdom. He didn't want any off-field mistake that would generate headlines for all the wrong reasons.

"Take care of yourselves; take care of each other. There are a lot of positive things to build off of. That's on me. The defense let this team down. That's on me. If we have to go with just eleven guys for sixty minutes, that's what we'll do."

He paused.

"L-E-O [love each other]. Is that clear?"

"Yes, sir."

And then they prayed.

## CHAPTER 17

# Virginia

TOM ALLEN SR. WASN'T THERE, AND IT HURT.
Allen's father was always there, at games, at many of the practices. He was a voice of encouragement and wisdom and love. It had been that way since the son had begun coaching two decades earlier.

Indiana was preparing for a trip to up-and-coming Virginia, and Tom Sr. was preparing for quadruple bypass heart surgery in Indianapolis. A family history of heart trouble, and 80 percent blockage in four heart arteries, made surgery necessary.

The son would coach against Virginia. There was no doubt about that. The elder Allen insisted on it.

Four days before kickoff, the younger Allen was in the War Room for a defensive staff meeting. After the meeting, he would head to Indianapolis to visit his father in the hospital ahead of surgery. Until then, he watched video of that morning's practice. He saw a linebacker playing tentatively. That couldn't happen.

"I don't know if he's injured," Allen said. "This isn't personal, but if this is how you practice, you can't play. This is a huge thing to me. He looks like an old man out there."

Cornerbacks coach Brandon Shelby saw, via Twitter, that Maryland had lost their starting quarterback to injury. He mentioned it to the group.

"That's the third starting quarterback to get lost for the season in the first weekend," Allen said.

Video images of practice flashed fast. They showed the scout offensive team giving the defense plays and looks of what to expect from Virginia.

"He needs to understand the fits," Allen said about a linebacker. Then he turned to defensive line coach Mark Hagen about the way the line had attacked a Virginia play.

"Talk me through this, Mark. Do you like it?"

Then Allen started and stopped the video multiple times.

"I don't understand what we're trying to do here," he said. "It's a total lack of awareness."

More video flashed. A cornerback hesitated when aggression was needed.

"Attack. Oh, Lord, help me," Shelby said and shifted his hat as if to shield his eyes from what he'd seen.

Then the Hoosiers began getting it right.

"That's good, good, good, good," Allen said. "That's encouraging. It means they understand what we're trying to accomplish."

For the first time since the meeting had begun, Allen smiled. A few minutes later, it was time to head to the hospital.

⊹⇒◎⇐⊹

Indiana coaches worried about the Virginia game from the moment they saw it on the schedule. Traveling to play a Power 5 conference team is always a challenge, especially for a traditionally struggling program such as Indiana. Add the fact it came days after such an emotional season opener against Ohio State, and only the most mature of teams could respond positively.

The Hoosiers did—and got some quarterback intrigue in the process.

Backup freshman quarterback Peyton Ramsey made his first big impression. He showed why he, rather than senior Richard Lagow, might be the guy to run the offense. Why? Because his dual-threat ability moved the chains in ways Lagow could not. Against Virginia,

Ramsey threw for 2 touchdowns, ran 26 yards for another score, and sparked the Hoosiers to a 34–17 victory.

"They had zero success in running," Virginia coach Bronco Mendenhall said, "and then [Ramsey] came in."

The quarterback change wasn't surprising given Tom Allen and Mike DeBord had said they would coach to what worked, especially when it included what they most wanted from their quarterback— the ability to run, throw, and stress defenses to the breaking point.

Ramsey broke Virginia.

That made a huge difference.

Ramsey, the son of a successful Cincinnati high school coach (Doug), was an off-the-bench catalyst. He went 16 for 20 for 173 yards, 2 touchdowns, and 0 interceptions. He also ran for 42 yards and that touchdown.

Compare that to Lagow's 3 for 10 for 24 yards and an interception. In other words, the quarterback change was a no-brainer.

"We planned on playing [Ramsey], and he came in and was moving the team," Allen said. "There was no reason to make a switch. It's not about me or the individual. It's about the team. It's L-E-O."

Ramsey completed his first 11 passes for 118 yards before finally missing. That's hard to do against any team, let alone one from a Power 5 Conference, which Virginia was as a member of the ACC.

Early Hoosier offensive mistakes were everywhere—dropped passes, a Lagow interception, J-Shun Harris catching a punt at the 2-yard line rather than letting it go into the end zone for a touchback. Enter Ramsey, who delivered a huge second-quarter boost—6-for-6 passing for 68 yards with a 29-yard touchdown to Simmie Cobbs and 6 runs for 39 yards, including a touchdown.

Combine Griffin Oakes's 51-yard, half-ending field goal (making him IU's all-time field goal leader, with 54) with a dominant defense that turned Virginia's offense into first-half mush (6 Cavalier punts, 4 first downs, and 111 total yards) and Harris bouncing back from his earlier mistake to return a punt 44 yards for a touchdown, and you had plenty of reasons for optimism.

The Hoosiers came in angry about their virtually nonexistent running game against Ohio State that produced just 17 yards on 27 carries. Yes, much of that reflected a Buckeye front seven that rated among America's best, while IU had three new offensive line starters. Still, the Hoosiers expected better.

Left tackle Coy Cronk blamed the line, not the running backs. Offensive line coach Darren Hiller basically said the same thing.

"It doesn't matter what we're trying to do," Hiller said, "whether we're throwing it, running it, whatever. It starts up front. I think we had two winning grades out of the five [offensive line] spots. If we're not winning all five, it's not going to be a good situation for us."

Meanwhile, Virginia showed run defense vulnerability in its season-opening win against William & Mary, allowing 168 yards. In other words, IU seemed poised for a strong running day.

It delivered to a point (121 yards on 41 carries), especially in the fourth quarter, when it ran off crucial time and yards, although not a score. Harris's punt return for a touchdown clinched the victory and, a few days later, earned him Big Ten special teams player of the week honors.

The Hoosiers showed poise and toughness, especially when a game-clinching, fourth-quarter fumble return for a touchdown by defensive end Robert McCray was wiped out by a targeting call on defensive end Greg Gooch.

That turned a 24-point lead into 10-point uncertainty. Then IU did what Allen had preached from the day he took over the previous December: they finished. As a result, Allen earned his first victory as a college head coach.

The first thing he thought about was his father.

"He's my hero," he said.

In the emotional postgame locker room, IU athletic director Fred Glass presented two game balls. The first went to the entire team for the way everyone responded after the tough Ohio State loss. The second game ball went to Allen for his first victory, which he gave to his father.

"I wouldn't be here if it wasn't for him," the younger Allen said.

As far as the game, Allen said, "To fight back from adversity like we did was unbelievable. Adversity is part of life. Sometimes life isn't fair, and you have to respond, and they did."

A few days later, more adversity hit.

The September 16 home game against Florida International was canceled because of the damage to the state of Florida caused by Hurricane Irma. Florida International would not be able to make the trip to Bloomington. The Hoosiers would get an unexpected—and unwanted—bye. Glass quickly found a replacement game with Charleston Southern on October 7. That date was originally set up as IU's bye week.

Hoosier coaches took advantage of the off weekend to hit the recruiting road. Players got some rest and prepared for a grueling stretch of playing for ten straight weeks.

IU needed to build momentum with Big Ten play set to resume. Next up: Georgia Southern.

## CHAPTER 18

# Georgia Southern

ALLEN SLOUCHED IN HIS CHAIR AT THE END OF A TABLE strewn with notepads, water bottles, food containers, and plastic cups. The War Room buzzed with serious talk, funny talk, the kind of talk you get among hardworking people who love what they do, and who love each other.

Allen steered the conversation to Georgia Southern and his concern about its cut-block preference. Cut blocking, also called chop blocking, is when an offensive player tries to knock down a defensive player by hitting at the knees.

"Take away their spirit fast," Allen said, then mentioned how Georgia Southern had pushed SEC powers Florida and Georgia to the limit in previous years.

Talk turned to the next day's practice.

"Team tackling," Allen said. "That's a big key."

Quality control specialist Jeff McInerney, whose focus was on special teams, mentioned a starburst formation. It's a trick kickoff return where a player catches the kickoff and turns his back to the kicking team while teammates gather around him so the kicking team doesn't know who has the ball. The ball can either be kept by the player who caught it or handed off to another player, and then everybody starts running, forcing the kicking team to figure out who has the ball.

The idea was to confuse the kicking team and generate a big return.

"I got it on video if you want to see it," McInerney said.

Offensive line coach Darren Hiller quickly cut in.

"Hey, that's my line!"

In fact, it was Hiller's line. It was one of his favorite phrases, and the room erupted into laughter.

Allen wanted to ratchet up the practice competition between the offense and defense based on first, second, and third downs. The winning group would get a reward.

"It should be something fun," Allen said.

Cornerbacks coach Brandon Shelby quickly cut in.

"We could have offensive and defensive linemen have to catch punts," he said with a smile.

Everybody laughed.

"We could have the losers run sprints," strength coach Keith Caton suggested. He wore a shirt that said "Being a part of something bigger than ourselves."

"Let's have something fun," Allen said.

They settled on the winners getting popsicles.

As the meeting ended, safeties coach Noah Joseph told Hiller, "You need to have confidence."

"I have a lot of confidence," Hiller said. "It's hard being this big without confidence."

The room again erupted in laughter.

Allen ended things with this thought: "Recruit. Recruit. Recruit."

⊷⊶

Indiana coaches didn't expect to have two weeks to prepare for Georgia Southern, but, then, no one expected Hurricane Irma to hit the state of Florida with category-5 force.

So here was offensive coordinator Mike DeBord, analyzing video and preparing offensive plans from his Memorial Stadium office. Behind him, windows looked out at the practice field. A large TV was mounted high on a wall. It was tied into his computer. DeBord started looking at Georgia Southern game video. He had a bunch of Georgia Southern games and plays to choose from. He focused on the Georgia Southern defense. He had cut-up videos of formations, down and distance, red zone, and blitzes. He looked for tendencies the Hoosiers could exploit. DeBord also considered his own offensive play-calling tendencies.

"You create tendencies to break tendencies is one approach," he said. "[Former Green Bay Packers coach] Mike Holmgrem didn't care about tendencies. He felt if you did it well enough, let the other team worry about stopping it. I like to know my tendencies and how I call a game."

Using the computer, DeBord could see how often he called a run or pass on first down and what play. On a certain formation, one was 51 percent pass, 49 percent run.

"You want efficient plays," he said. "On first down, that's four or more yards. On third down, it's whatever is needed for a first down.

"I'm a meat-and-potatoes play-caller. We have others on the staff who are creative. I push for execution. Let's block and execute."

DeBord pointed to his computer and mentioned Alex Agassi, the former Purdue head football coach.

"At the end of his career, he used to hang around the Michigan football offices. He would say, 'You coaches are messing football up. We never had computers or practice film. We never had cutups.'"

DeBord clicked on more video.

"As coaches, we put in a lot more hours now. People have no idea how complicated this game is."

It was time for an offensive meeting. Like the defense, there were code words that made sense only to those on the inside, terms such as "Dexter" and "Texas" and "Sonic." The coaches watched video, lots of video replayed over and over. One sequence showed offensive lineman Coy Cronk blocking a defensive lineman then hustling to make blocks in the secondary when most offensive linemen would have stopped.

"I love 54," offensive line coach Darren Hiller said, a reference to Coy's uniform number. "He's busting his tail. It's just ingrained in him. He's awesome."

The other offensive coaches nodded in agreement. More practice video followed . . . and more replays. DeBord noticed a seldom-used player and commented on his lack of playing time.

"He's blessed with my speed," DeBord said. "I'm kidding. I didn't say that. I don't think he lacks toughness. He can help us, but he can't play tight end. Let's make him an offensive lineman. He might help us down the road."

More practice video flashed by. DeBord shook his head.

"I don't understand these guys. Look at the left guard here. Who's going to block the guy if you don't?"

No one answered. Then wide receivers coach Grant Heard went for humor.

"I just hit my funny bone, and it's not that funny."

⟿ ⟾

Another staff meeting loomed, and the War Room was decorated in pink and white balloons, with a pink-and-white "Happy Birthday" sign. It was staff member Jim Nelson's birthday.

Allen was happy about the morning practice but wanted more.

"We want them to keep fighting. Everything will be a challenge. Make it what we want it to be. Everything has to be at a fever pitch."

And then . . . "We have some great scout guys. They help us win. They're huge for our success."

Conversation switched to Florida's dramatic last-second victory over Tennessee a couple of days earlier. With the score tied at 20–20, Florida quarterback Feleipe Franks hit receiver Tyrie Cleveland for a 63-yard, game-winning touchdown pass on the game's final play.

"You need to know how far the quarterback can throw," Allen said. "Can he get it to the end zone? If not, look for the pitch play. We need to learn from that. It could happen to us."

⟿ ⟾

Victory was predicated on IU's ability to run. It was about being more man than the other guy, about the offensive line growing up and a freshman tailback settling in. Oh, and thriving after an unexpected bye.

Offensive line coach Darren Hiller offered perspective. Against Ohio State, two guys on the offensive line graded out at a winning level. The second game, it was three offensive linemen getting a winning grade.

"Defensive linemen are hard to block," Hiller said. "We have to keep on our craft. It's about getting more comfortable. We've got to get better at running. We've got to do it."

Beyond that, IU hadn't played in two weeks because of the cancelation of the Florida International game due to complications from Hurricane Irma. That meant coach Tom Allen had an extra week to stew over the lack of defensive takeaways. The goal was to get at least three in every game. IU had zero in its first two games.

Allen mentioned that, and a lot more, to the Hoosiers. The result: they got those 3 turnovers (including a defensive score on defensive back Andre Brown's interception return for a TD), found the running game, delivered special teams excitement (J-Shun Harris returned a punt 70 yards for a touchdown), scored on long pass plays, and won big over outgunned Georgia Southern, 52–17. Dominance was everywhere you looked. Indiana produced explosion plays on offense, defense, and special teams.

The two straight wins came with an average victory margin of 32 points. Holding Virginia and Georgia Southern to 17 points each met another defensive goal. In other words, life was cream 'n' crimson good.

"We started fast and finished strong," Allen said. "That's something we really emphasized. We want to play at a consistent high level. That's the key."

Allen kept pushing that theme. Even when the Hoosiers were in full blowout mode in the fourth quarter, he didn't dial back the intensity. The disappointment from big games nearly won remained relentlessly fresh—and motivating.

"I hate sloppy finishes," Allen said. "I want consistent performance. That's what we're shooting for. That's what great teams do. They perform to their standard. If you can't play to our standard, we're going to run you right over. We haven't always done that in the past. I'm aware of that. We're trying to change that."

A big change featured freshman tailback Morgan Ellison, who in his first college start showed flashes reminiscent of Hoosier legend Anthony Thompson. The six-one, 225-pound Ellison rushed for 186 yards on 25 carries. It was the fourth-most yards ever by a true Hoosier freshman. Thompson has the record with 207 yards.

"I got a couple of good runs and thought, 'Let's keep going, let's keep going,'" Ellison said. "I thought it was my time, honestly."

His time was earned starting in August camp, when he punished would-be tacklers as if he were wearing pads. The problem? He wasn't wearing pads.

"I used to play rugby, so I'm used to not wearing pads," he said. "[Teammates] got upset in camp. They said, 'You can't be running like that,' and 'You're going to hurt yourself.'"

Ellison's motivation came from missing most of his high school sophomore and junior seasons because of leg injuries. He came back with a 1,841-yard, 29-touchdown senior year, but the recruiting damage had been done. A flurry of big-time scholarship offers never came. So when Ellison arrived at IU's fall camp, he was determined to make a big impression.

"I thought I had to prove something after breaking my legs twice in high school."

Against Georgia Southern, Ellison benefited from an offensive adjustment designed to spark the running game.

"We knew [Georgia Southern's] defensive line was their strength," Allen said. "We knew it would be tough. We tried to spread them out and run out of that look. It was very efficient."

Georgia Southern (0–3) was once a lower-level national power, winning six national titles and throwing scares into any major college team they played. That fear was gone. The Hoosiers jumped to a 31–0 lead in less than twenty football minutes. They punished the

Eagles' triple-option rushing attack. They hammered with the run, staggered via more Harris punt return spectacle.

Harris returned a first-quarter punt for a touchdown. It was the second straight game he scored on a punt return to tie IU's single-season record set by Rob Turner in 1990. Two other Hoosiers have returned two punts for touchdowns in a season: Mitchell Paige (2015) and Larry Highbaugh (1969).

In three games, Harris, who won Big Ten special teams player of the week honors for his Virginia performance (he had 44- and 42-yard punt returns), had returned 7 punts for 183 yards. He returned two punts for 74 yards on two returns against Georgia Southern. He had missed the previous two seasons because of knee injuries.

"How about J-Shun?" Allen said. "That kid is unreal. They're probably going to quit punting to him. He's making them pay. What a great story."

The quarterback rotation of Richard Lagow and Peyton Ramsey combined for 11-of-21 passing for 185 yards. Both players threw touchdown passes. Lagow connected with tight end Ian Thomas for 71 yards. Ramsey hit tailback Devonte Williams with a 42-yard score.

Lagow injured his leg on his third-quarter touchdown pass. He didn't return, but Allen said he could have.

"We wanted to make sure we protected him," Allen said.

IU's defense sprung some leaks—Georgia Southern totaled 375 yards, 173 more than their average, with 133 coming by the pass—but Allen could live with that.

"This [Georgia Southern offensive] scheme will make you lose sleep at night," he said. "You're so focused on the run. The formations they did out of it were totally new. We still thought we had it fixed. It's just eye discipline. It was the stinking play-action option passes. We may never see that the rest of the year, so there's really no reason to be concerned."

IU forced 3 fumbles, with the big one coming from defensive back Andre Brown, who returned it 22 yards for a fourth-quarter touchdown to end the scoring.

The Hoosiers entered the game without a takeaway.

"Our goal is three a game," Allen said. "I make such a big deal about takeaways, so I get really upset and frustrated when we don't get them. The Andre Brown one was great. He just took the ball away. We work on that all the time. We talk that if you want to be a great defense, you've got to score on defense. Andre finished well. That's what we want."

On a day for dominance, that's what mattered most.

## CHAPTER 19

# Penn State

TOM ALLEN SENSED TROUBLE FOUR DAYS BEFORE IT
happened.

The Hoosiers had practiced sluggishly. They lacked the necessary fire crucial to success. This was bad even if they were preparing
to play a patsy. That they would travel to powerhouse Penn State,
which had one of the nation's best offenses and two of the best players, was beyond concerning.

Allen took the lead in the War Room

"I thought they look a little tired," he said after a Tuesday practice.
"Gooch had tremendous energy, as usual."

That was senior defensive end Greg Gooch, who had emerged as
a difference-making leader as well as player.

"Make sure your guys are taking care of themselves," Allen told
his staff. "Stay on your guys. Make sure they're living right. We can't
take a tired team to Penn State." He paused. "Convince them to get
their rest. What I saw wasn't good enough."

Defensive line coach Mark Hagen nodded in agreement.

"It boils down to a choice. Get to bed and get rest."

Strength coach Keith Caton mentioned the recent hot tempera-
tures. He said he'd emphasize to players the importance of sleep
and hydration.

Allen eyed his coaches. "We're not going to take a tired team to
Penn State. It's a long game. I get that. We've got to get their bodies
back. Be on top of your guys."

Beyond possible fatigue, injuries were mounting. Cornerback A'Shon Riggins and defensive back Marcelino Ball were out with injuries. Offensive lineman Simon Stepaniak had missed the Georgia Southern game but was ready for the Nittany Lions.

Defensive coaches focused on how to stop Penn State tailback Saquon Barkley and quarterback Trace McSorley, two of the nation's best players.

Safeties coach Noah Joseph asked, "Are we foolish to try to take Barkley one on one? I'm just talking out loud. He'll make us miss some. We have to make tackles."

As it turned out, the Hoosiers did.

⊷⟹⟸⊶

Early against Penn State, returner J-Shun Harris was knocked out of the game from a big hit. He fumbled on the play. The Nittany Lions recovered and returned it for a touchdown. That was part of a disastrous start. The Hoosiers opened by giving up a 98-yard kickoff return for a touchdown to Barkley. They trailed 28–0 after the first quarter.

IU got second-quarter momentum from Ricky Brookins's 2-yard touchdown run and Peyton Ramsey's 18-yard scoring pass to Simmie Cobbs. By halftime, the Hoosiers trailed 28–14 with a comeback chance.

The Nittany Lions controlled the second half and won 45–14. Indiana stopped the run, holding the Nittany Lions to just 39 rushing yards on 37 carries. Barkley managed just 56 yards on 20 carries.

The Hoosiers had solid offensive balance with 177 rushing yards, 175 passing yards. But the big question came at quarterback. After starting the first four games, Lagow's status was in question. Against Penn State, Lagow was 7-for-15 for 97 yards. Ramsey was 8-for-17 for 78 yards, a touchdown, and an interception. He'd also rushed for 53 yards.

For the season, Ramsey had shown better accuracy along with the better running. While Lagow had burned Ohio State for 40 completions, 410 passing yards, and 3 touchdowns, he couldn't sustain that consistency level.

Coaches had a decision to make. Should they stay with Lagow or turn to Ramsey and live with the youthful mistakes sure to occur because they needed his dual-threat advantage and his beyond-his-years poise (the benefit of being the son of a successful high school coach, Doug Ramsey at Cincinnati Elder)? If they made the switch, Ramsey would have what was in essence a tune-up game to get ready for Big Ten battles. Charleston Southern was next. It was a lower-division team not close to IU's level in scholarships, talent, resources, or experience. Ramsey would have a chance for early starting experience, success, and confidence-building.

Allen and offensive coordinator Mike DeBord met with this overriding thought: Who would give IU the best chance to win, now and in the future? The choice was made: Ramsey.

CHAPTER 20

# Charleston Southern

COACHES GATHERED IN THE WAR ROOM, AND THE NUMBER-
one focus was on the quarterback change.

How could it not?

Perhaps no position in any sport at any level is as important as
quarterback, and moving from a senior with NFL potential to a
redshirt freshman was a risk.

Or was it?

For Allen and DeBord, the potential reward made all the
difference.

Lagow and Ramsey were told the Sunday night after the Penn
State game. The Hoosiers had Monday off, so the first practice with
the new arrangement came that Tuesday morning. Afterward, Allen asked quarterbacks coach Nick Sheridan how Lagow handled
his demotion.

"He was fine," Sheridan said. "The body language was a little
down. There was a level of embarrassment. He'll be fine."

Sheridan leaned forward in his seat. "One thing I took from it
was the level of trust they have in you, Coach. They'll support the
decision."

Allen fidgeted uncomfortably in his chair. It had not been an easy
decision for him to make. No coach cared more about his players
than he did, especially a player who had worked as hard as Lagow.

"I know it's hard," Allen said. "It's a tough decision. The players
believe in Peyton. He works hard. He does everything right."

Allen drew on a notepad.

"I feel good about the decision."

More drawing.

"I wanted it for Rich. It's done. Let's roll."

As so they did, switching the discussion to the next day's practice and an emphasis on ball security. Allen wanted drills focused on ball security for the offense and takeaways for the defense. Then he mentioned a player who got him so annoyed that Allen thought about using colorful vocabulary. That's big because Allen never used colorful vocabulary.

"I about did cuss," he said, "but then I thought, *He's not going to make me cuss.*"

Offensive line coach Darren Hiller brought up one of his offensive linemen, six-foot-six, 305-pound junior Delroy Baker.

"He has a small dog," Hiller said. "You can put it in a purse. It fits in your hand."

"I thought it was his girlfriend's dog?" a coach asked.

"No. It's his," Hiller said.

Left unsaid was the contrast of a person as big and powerful as Baker having a tiny dog.

Allen switched the topic back to Charleston Southern.

"It's about making plays," he said. "Make the play when it counts."

Allen offered a challenge of the day as a way to motivate and inspire.

"When things are tough and don't make sense, God tells you to trust him. It's a mind-set. It's how you look at life. When things go wrong, trust in something bigger than you. When you have adversity, be thankful for what you do have."

Then he turned football specific.

"Continue to motivate your guys," he said. "Get them to elevate. Keep them focused. We want to dominate and elevate, no matter who is in the game."

Allen mentioned a player newly put on the kickoff team. The unit's number-one priority: tackle the kick returner as close to his own goal line as possible. During practice, the player didn't know what to do or who to look for. That was a problem.

"He was just running down the field as fast as he could," Allen said. "Don't assume [players know what they are doing]. He had no clue what to do. He didn't have his eyes in the right spot. "I had to tell him, 'Tackle the runner; don't block for him.' This is the kickoff coverage team." Allen tried not to laugh. He looked across the room. "Take it where we need to take it. Get them ready."

⋆⟫⟨⋆

A monsoon rain couldn't wreck IU's perfect outcome following an imperfect scheduling adjustment. Neither could an outgunned Charleston Southern that got $500,000, plus $150,000 in travel expenses for the opportunity to get crushed.

And the Hoosiers did crush—with the kind of defense they hadn't produced in a generation and a quarterback starting debut from Peyton Ramsey that suggested big things were coming. The 27–0 victory held this reality: the lower-level Bucs had twenty fewer scholarships and not close to the resources needed to compete on the road against a Big Ten team.

Still, domination was the goal, and the Hoosiers more than delivered, something that hadn't always happened in cream 'n' crimson history against inferior opponents.

First, some background. IU had planned for a bye on the first Saturday in October. The original schedule had the break coming five weeks into the season. It would provide some much-needed time off before powerhouse Michigan came to Memorial Stadium. With students and many Bloomington residents out because of fall break, it was well timed to avoid a potential game attendance hit.

Hurricane Irma rocked those plans.

The aftermath of that devastating storm forced the cancelation of the September 16 Florida International game and left athletic director Fred Glass scrambling to find a replacement game. The Hoosiers' only date was October 7.

The problem: by playing then, the Hoosiers would end the season by playing ten straight weeks. That would push their depth to the limit and leave them potentially vulnerable to injury and wear and tear. Still, school officials considered that better than only playing eleven games and losing a home contest. Glass went to work, and in just a couple of days, he found an opponent. Charleston Southern would come to Memorial Stadium.

The Buccaneers were an FCS (Football Championship Subdivision) power with consecutive trips to the national playoffs. They had basically averaged nine victories a year for the previous four seasons. They were favored to win the Big South Conference title for the third straight season. However, they came in with a 0–19 record against FBS (Football Bowl Subdivision) teams such as Indiana.

Charleston Southern had a new coach in Mark Tucker and a run-dominant triple-option offense similar to what IU had faced against Georgia Southern. After losing their first two games 49–0 at Mississippi State (gaining just 2 first downs and only 33 yards of total offense) and 19–17 at Elon, the Buccaneers had bounced back to beat Point University 66–0 and Mississippi Valley State 58–7.

What did this mean against the Hoosiers? Not much, as it turned out.

Again, it was the perfect scenario, especially for a defense striving to reach top-twenty-five-in-the-nation status (playing two of the nation's top offenses in Ohio State and Penn State skewed the early numbers) and a young quarterback needing experience to thrive in upcoming challenges. The shutout mattered.

"It's awesome," defensive end Jacob Robinson said.

The Hoosiers squeezed the life out of the Bucs' run-dominant offense in ways that hadn't been seen in a generation.

"The shutout was our number-one goal," Robinson said. "We'd talked a lot this week about dominating. That was our word: dominate."

Mission accomplished. Charleston Southern (2–3) never came close to scoring. The Bucs only got into IU territory four times.

The closest they came to the end zone was the Hoosier 31-yard line, and that was in the first quarter. Beyond that, the Bucs totaled just 134 yards, all by the run. They punted 12 times.

Yes, Charleston Southern reminded no one of, say, Ohio State. Still, IU had a history of not playing to its potential against struggling teams. Tom Allen was determined to change that. He yearned for zeros by opponents' names. He got what he wanted: the Bucs had zero points, zero passing yards, and zero completions.

"Every win is a big win," he said. "You don't take anything for granted. Anytime you can shut somebody out, I don't care who they are, it's not easy to do. It's a big deal."

The last time IU had a shutout was in 1993, when it blanked Michigan State 10–0.

This was the seventh time the Hoosiers have held a team without a completion (the Bucs were 0-for-10), but it was not a school record for fewest passing yards. Purdue had minus-2 yards against IU in 1945, the year the Hoosiers won the Big Ten title.

For a program that had been a defensive disaster until Allen showed up the previous season, this was big-time good.

"[A shutout] is big for the program and our defense," defensive lineman Mike Barwick Jr. said. "We're on the up and up."

The Hoosiers were way up despite a fierce second-half rain and sitting out key players such as defensive backs Marcelino Ball, A'Shon Riggins, punt returner J-Shun Harris, receiver Donavan Hale, tight end Ian Thomas, defensive lineman Nate Hoff, and offensive linemen Simon Stepaniak because of injuries.

Backups such as cornerback LaDamion Hunt, tight end Ryan Watercutter, Barwick, linebacker Mike McGinnis, and receiver Ty Fryfogle saw significant action.

"I think it's extremely valuable," Allen said, "because practice reps are important, but they're not the same as game-day reps. We played a whole bunch of guys on both sides of the ball, and the more they play, the better they'll get. There were a lot of positives to build off of."

It started with Ramsey, who showed he was more than ready for his first college start. He was 32 for 41 for 321 yards, 2 touchdowns, and an interception. He also rushed for 54 yards and recovered a fumble in the end zone for a touchdown. Ramsey was the first freshman quarterback at IU to surpass 300 passing yards since Kellen Lewis did it against Minnesota in 2006. For comparison, Ramsey had thrown for 316 yards total in the four previous games as the backup.

Credit much of that to offensive coordinator Mike DeBord, who tweaked the offense to maximize Ramsey's dual-threat ability. That included allowing him to throw from outside the pocket and mixing short passes and slants.

"I've played in the last four games, so it wasn't new to be out there," Ramsey said, "but it was a huge confidence boost to get a win."

This was exactly what Allen hoped for after naming him the starter six days earlier.

"I wanted him to have the whole week to deal with that, talk to the media, and prepare accordingly," Allen said. "To not come off the bench like he'd done. I thought that was important.

"He seemed very calm. He ran things. He protected the ball. To get this game under his belt and go back to Big Ten play was really important."

A big target was freshman receiver Taysir Mack, who caught seven passes for 111 yards and a touchdown. He was the first cream 'n' crimson freshman to break 100 receiving yards since Tandon Doss in 2008. This reflected the overall program development Allen wanted to see.

"My thing is this: we want to build a team that plays to the strength of our team, and that's from a defensive perspective, special teams perspective, and the offense. All three working together to win games.

"When you play great defense and you're good on special teams, then you want to control the ball from a tempo perspective, whether you need to go fast, slow, whatever you need to do to win."

So Indiana won, and if it didn't come against a Big Ten-caliber opponent, that didn't diminish the sense of accomplishment.

"It takes a lot of work to win," Allen said. "This was a team we were supposed to beat, and we did. We realize what we have, and [we] have to get ready for [Michigan]."

CHAPTER 21

# Michigan

POWERHOUSE MICHIGAN LOOMED, AND HOOSIER COACHES
saw vulnerability. The defense-minded Wolverines (4–1) were
coming off a 14–10 home loss to rival Michigan State in which
they showed significant offensive flaws. Coaches also saw a big
challenge—Michigan had shown eighteen different looks on their
defensive front against Michigan State, a complexity that added to
the preparation burden.

Rain forced Tuesday morning practice into the Mellencamp
Pavilion, IU's indoor training facility, and coaches pushed the
intensity.

"Go run the play," Allen shouted through a bullhorn as the number-one defense faced the scout team offense.

"You're lunging," safeties coach Noah Joseph yelled. "Just go and
make the tackle."

When defensive lineman Jerome Johnson did, Allen was quick
with praise.

"Way to recognize it. That's the way, Ninety-eight."

And then Allen ratcheted up his intensity.

"Compete! Compete! Compete! You have to finish. It's a habit.
Defense must pressure. Offense must protect. Be in position to
make a play. You've got to finish!"

Later, in the staff meeting, Allen sought input. He didn't want
a bunch of yes-men afraid to speak the truth. Defensive line coach
Mark Hagen was no yes-man. He would speak up if necessary.

"Any thoughts?" Allen asked.

"I thought practice was too long," Hagen said. "It was twenty minutes too long. I'm just being honest."

"I don't know that I agree with that," Allen said. "We've got to get the [backups] reps."

Hagen wasn't convinced.

"I've been around teams that won on Tuesday and had nothing in the tank on Saturday," he said.

Allen looked around the room. "Anybody agree with that?"

"I agree," strength coach Keith Caton said.

Allen is big on player development and maximizing practice time, especially with NCAA rules limiting that to twenty hours a week. It requires a challenging balancing act.

"I know the walk-through went long," Allen conceded. "I agree, but we have to get reps."

"If guys are acting tired," Joseph said, "make sure they're getting the right nutrition."

The coaches planned the next day's practice. Offensive coordinator Mike DeBord wanted extra work on third down plays because of the complexity of Michigan's defense.

Talk turned to recruiting. A big crowd was expected at Memorial Stadium because of Michigan's appearance and the fact it was IU's homecoming game. Coaches had planned for plenty of official and unofficial visits from recruits.

Allen ended things with a final practice thought:

"Make sure we maximize our time because of the volume on both sides of the ball [from Michigan]."

Later that day, DeBord talked about the challenges Michigan's fierce defense presented (the Wolverines used multiple formations and looks designed to confuse the most veteran of quarterbacks, let alone Ramsey, a freshman making just his second start) and how he planned to attack it. Michigan defensive coordinator Don Brown was one of the best at what he did. He had directed the nation's best defense in 2015 at Boston College and in 2016 at Michigan. For 2017, the Wolverines again led the nation in defense entering the Indiana game.

DeBord and his staff had a long Monday night meeting on how to handle Michigan's many blitzes and alignments. Coaches looked at first and second downs and the formations IU would use against the formations Michigan had shown on first and second downs. The Wolverines used a *lot* of formations, more than twenty, which is why DeBord talked about the complexity challenge. Then Hoosier coaches did the same thing for third downs and red zone plays. They did that for the entire game plan.

"We look at personnel, especially in man coverage," DeBord said. "Who do we need to attack in man coverage? How we'll attack them. Every pass we have has to be good against the coverages they play. They play a large majority of man defense, but if they jump into cover two [a zone defense where the two safeties drop back about 13 yards to cover deep passes], then we have to have answers for the quarterback. We go through all of that."

One thing was clear: Michigan would blitz a lot while attacking the receivers with man-to-man coverage, which would put Ramsey under nonstop duress.

"Our passing game has to be good against man-free coverage," DeBord said. "We have to do a great job with blitz pickup. They do multiple blitzes. There's a lot of one time of this blitz, one time of that blitz. We have to continue to work all that in the run-and-pass game.

"It takes coach preparation and then preparation on the practice field with walk-throughs and then live reps [with the scout team pretending to be Michigan's defense]. You've got to rep it all and be ready for it."

The veteran DeBord embraced the challenge. "It's a challenge every week. Defenses are multiple every week. And when you're going against probably the best defense in the country, it's a great challenge. You've got to be able to attack. You have to be thorough in your preparation. You can't leave anything to chance."

Allen felt the same way against a vulnerable Michigan offense that had scored just 10 points the previous week in a home loss to rival Michigan State, although a driving rainstorm and 5 turnovers were also contributing factors. Allen's plan was to target the Wolverines' offensive line.

"That's an area that's not one of their strengths. That's something we have to take advantage of. They also have a quarterback [John O'Korn, who'd thrown 1 touchdown pass and 4 interceptions] who hasn't always handled a variety of looks. We can affect him by showing him one thing, play something else. We can affect him with pressure. We can force him into mistakes. We need to create takeaways, and I think he can be the catalyst for that if we do it right."

Like the defense, the Michigan offense featured plenty of complexity with different formations and looks. Allen's strategy: "Go simpler. The more they do," he said, "the less you do. In order to still play fast, you have to do less things and let their multiplicity fit your multiplicity. We'll have concepts to match their concepts. We'll look a little bit different because they look different, but if you follow our rules, it's not hard for our guys."

Allen said his biggest concern was "them imposing their size on us and wearing us down by just running the ball. Running the ball and making us gang up on that and then throwing it over our heads."

⊶⊜⊷

Allen hit emotional overload. Sometimes tough guys do cry. Can you blame him?

The Hoosiers had pushed No. 17 Michigan to the brink. They had overcome enough adversity to break a less mentally tough team. They'd faced a series of questionable officiating calls, just as they had so many times before in the last forty years against Michigan. The perception of those calls had once again caused cynics to see conspiracy at work involving unknown elements, reaching to the upper levels of the Big Ten, determined to ensure teams such as Ohio State, Michigan, and Penn State would forever get the necessary breaks.

In the end, conspiracy didn't beat Indiana. Wolverine overtime playmaking and IU's inability to counter did.

So when sixty minutes of football action was finished, followed by an overtime period that left the Memorial Stadium scoreboard displaying the 27–20 lost-again truth, after giving a riveting locker room speech to his players, Allen broke down. It happened just before he did the postgame radio show. It happened again after doing his postgame press conference with wife Tracy at his side.

Once again, the Hoosiers were so close. Despite all the effort and planning and belief, the losing streak to Michigan that had begun in 1987 remained. It hurt. You bet it did.

And yet . . .

"The positive is we fought our tails off and tied the game, went to overtime, and had a chance to beat a top-twenty team," Allen said in the postgame press conference. "I'm proud of our team for that, but my heart breaks for these guys because they have worked so hard, and they believe so much, and they deserve to come out with a win. We've got to find a way to make those plays.

"Life isn't always about getting everything you want. It's about learning and creating a character and a resolve that will allow you to face any challenge. We're building men here. Then we're going to win."

IU trailed 13–0 late in the second quarter. It trailed 20–10 late in the fourth quarter. It faced a Wolverine defense that had turned offenses into mush, one that had allowed zero fourth-quarter points all season. And then, after having scored a fourth-quarter touchdown, the Hoosiers had apparently recovered an onside kick—thanks to spectacular execution from kicker Griffin Oakes and receiver Simmie Cobbs—only to have it reversed by official review.

Despite all that, the Hoosiers got the ball back one last time, forced overtime on Oakes's last-second field goal, and gave themselves a chance. Then, as it had so many times, the chance was gone.

Still, Allen found the silver lining. "It creates resolve," he said. "It creates a toughness and a fight. Stronger and tighter than ever. That's what it creates. There ain't no feeling sorry for nobody. This team has too much to them. There's too much love. Too much fight. Too much grit. There's too much invested.

"The average person would think that it would frustrate you. That's not how we're built. That's not how I'm wired. That's not how we're wired. That's not how this team will respond."

That's the overview.

Here are the specifics.

⊷═◉═⊷

So much seemed possible. So much was possible.

Michigan arrived with uncertainty. The offensive line had been a sieve the previous week in a home loss against rival Michigan State. Coach Jim Harbaugh was criticized for play-calling that put too much of a burden on quarterback John O'Korn and not enough on tailback Ty Isaac. And the red-zone offense was miserable, generating just 5 touchdowns in 15 opportunities, one of the worst rates in the country.

The Wolverines had struggled with their quarterback play all season. O'Korn and Wilton Speight, the starter until being sidelined with a back injury, had completed just 55.6 percent of their passes with 4 touchdowns and 6 interceptions.

Allen's defensive game plan was simple—attack that offensive line and force O'Korn into mistakes (he had thrown 3 interceptions against Michigan State). Defensively, Michigan was a beast. It led the nation with just 213 total yards allowed a game. It gave up 13.6 points, second best in the Big Ten. The Wolverines would attack youthful quarterback Peyton Ramsey with pressure, deception, and aggression. Could he hold up? Would the offensive line and running game allow him to hold up?

IU blinked first.

Michigan got a pair of Quinn Nordin field goals, from 40 and 38 yards, to take a 6–0 lead early in the second quarter. The Hoosiers' defense stiffened and was positioned for a key stop. But on third and long midway through the second quarter, O'Korn eluded a seemingly certain sack to complete a 17-yard pass (his longest of the game) for a big first down. That led to tailback Karan Higdon's 12-yard touchdown run and a 13–0 lead.

Indiana battled back. It got an Oakes 32-yard field goal just before halftime to make it 13–3.

Then IU officials, in their never-ending quest to boost entertainment bang for the buck, had a halftime promotion where pro golfer and Indiana alum Shaun Micheel, the 2003 PGA champ (through 2017, it remained his only PGA Tour victory), tried to land a golf ball from the Memorial Stadium patio in front of athletic director Fred Glass's office onto the big IU logo in the center of the field. If he did, a trip to Myrtle Beach would be awarded to a lucky contest participant.

Micheel came close but missed. There was no prize winner.

Afterward, the Hoosiers kept fighting. They got an early third-quarter 8-yard TD run from tailback Morgan Ellison to cut the lead to 13–10.

Michigan came back with Higdon's 59-yard fourth-quarter touchdown run to go ahead by 10 points.

The Hoosiers seemed finished. They were not. Ramsey hit freshman receiver Whop Philyor with an 8-yard touchdown pass with just 3:27 left in regulation. Then came the onside kick, which was recovered and then ruled not.

It was the third time officiating injustice seemed to strike the Hoosiers. Earlier, Cobbs had caught a 64-yard pass after being shoved out of bounds by a Michigan defender, only to have officials rule it incomplete after review. They said Cobbs hadn't yet reestablished in-bounds position before making the catch. Also, an interception by cornerback Rashard Fant was wiped out after officials ruled pass interference on him despite little visible evidence of that.

No matter. Allen told an upset Oakes to stay focused after the missed onside kick because he'd get another chance. Allen fired up the defense to get a stop.

The defense did. Michigan went three and out and punted. Ramsey drove the Hoosiers from their own 30-yard line into field goal range, and as time expired, Oakes hit a 46-yard field goal to force overtime.

After sixty minutes of drama, IU had earned a reboot. All that was left was the key element Allen had preached since taking over the program: finish.

⋆⇢═◉═⇠⋆

College overtime gives both teams a chance with first and ten at the 25-yard line. Teams play as many overtimes as necessary to determine a winner. If it goes into a third overtime, teams have to go for 2-point conversions on touchdowns. The record for most overtime sessions was seven.

IU won the overtime toss and elected to play defense. That would give them the chance to see exactly what they would do on their possession. Knowledge came fast. On Michigan's first play, Higdon was on the verge of a big running loss. But he avoided tacklers, got to the outside, and ran 25 yards for a touchdown. A defense that had come through for so long failed to deliver. It was up to the offense.

A Michigan pass interference penalty and runs of 9 yards by Ramsey and 2 by Ellison gave IU a first down at the Michigan 1-yard line. The Hoosiers needed a touchdown to force a second overtime period.

It never came.

Two runs up the middle, one by Ellison, one by Ramsey, into the heart of one of the nation's best defenses resulted in a loss of 3 yards. Two roll-out passes to the left, forcing the right-handed Ramsey to throw across his body, produced a miss to an open J-Shun Harris and then, on the game's final play, an interception.

The game—and a huge opportunity—was lost.

Criticism came hard and fast, from young and old, male and female, knowledgeable fans and those who thought they were. In this view, the overtime play calling for those final four plays was—to be politically correct—unfortunate. In stronger terms, it was bleeping lousy.

Not surprisingly, offensive coordinator Mike DeBord, the man who made the calls, did not agree. When asked at his weekly press conference two days later if he'd do anything differently, DeBord said, "Nope. Not at all." Then he elaborated. "Nobody is harder on play calling than I am on myself. Tom [Allen] looked at it as well. The plays were there. We have to do a better job of executing those. They were base calls, basically.

"When I talk about execution, I'm talking about that we have to coach those plays better. We went back at it [the day after the game in practice] and worked on the fundamentals of those plays. We'll be better at them.

"I looked at every one of them. I thought they were good calls."

DeBord was specifically asked about having Ramsey rolling out to throw rather than dropping back.

"With play calling, after the play is called, everybody is, 'Why didn't you do this or do that?'" DeBord said. "What if we would have dropped back and taken the sack? Then you'd hear, 'Why didn't you sprint out?'

"Peyton is a guy who can throw on the run. He's demonstrated that in practice. He's done it in games. We were trying to get Simmie in motion [on fourth down]. I'm not going to get into the officiating, that's not my role, but the play didn't develop like we wanted it to."

In fact, the first three calls could have produced a touchdown. DeBord twice called running plays where Ramsey had to read the defense to see which play would work best. On first down, if he had faked to Ellison and run, he likely would have scored. On third down, if he had given the ball to Ellison, the tailback likely would have scored.

Ramsey missed an open Harris on second down, not because he was incapable of throwing accurately across his body, as some suggested, but because he just threw a bad pass. Bottom line, you had a young quarterback in a pressure-packed moment who made a few mistakes. Figure he'll be better in the future because of them.

In the end, Michigan rushed for 271 yards and averaged 6.1 yards a carry. Higdon was the difference with his scoring runs of 59 and 25 yards.

Ellison had a team-leading 68 rushing yards, with 31 coming on one play. Ramsey was 20 for 41 for 178 yards, 1 touchdown, and 2 interceptions. Cobbs was targeted 10 times but managed just 4 catches for 39 yards. Slot receiver Luke Timian had a career-high 95 receiving yards on 7 catches.

Free safety Chase Dutra had 13 tackles, while husky Tony Fields (7 tackles) and cornerback Rashard Fant (4 tackles and a pass breakup) were named defensive players of the game by coaches.

It wasn't enough.

In the aftermath, Hoosier players pushed perspective.

"It's frustrating," All-America linebacker Tegray Scales said. "All that work throughout the week and the offseason. These are close games you want to win, and you lose. It never feels good, but you can't keep your head down.

"We are right there. We didn't win, but we see what we're capable of."

## CHAPTER 22

# Michigan State

A CRISP OCTOBER TUESDAY PRACTICE HAD STRIPPING ON Hoosier defensive minds.

Strip the ball.

Rake the ball.

Take it, intercept it, do whatever was necessary to get the bleeping thing away from the offense.

"Take the ball from them," Tom Allen shouted via bullhorn emphasis.

A play was made. Cornerback Rashard Fant broke up a pass.

"Well done," Allen shouted. "Nice job, Number Sixteen [Fant]. Great position. Now you've gotta play."

Practice headed toward its conclusion. A running back burst through for a big gain.

"Wrap him up and strip the ball," Allen shouted. "You have to make the tackle!"

Safeties coach Noah Joseph flashed in with quick instructions: "Make something happen!"

Linebacker Reakwon Jones intercepted a pass. A few moments later, safety Zeke Walker got an interception.

"Keep taking it from them!" Allen shouted.

Allen was on the prowl. He demanded takeaways, and the Hoosiers hadn't delivered. It wasn't from lack of effort. Sometimes it was bad breaks or odd officiating calls or the whims of an ever-changing game.

Still . . .

After six games, IU ranked last in the Big Ten with just 4 take-aways—3 fumble recoveries and 1 interception. Northwestern was next to last with 8. Penn State led the conference with 17. So take-away emphasis was a weeklong practice theme.

"We're focusing on it," senior defensive back Tony Fields said. "It's taking the ball away, stripping it. Getting interceptions. It comes down to technique and trusting your responsibility. When you see something, attack. We have to get back into those habits. We talk about it all the time. I expect that to change. It's somebody ripping at the football. Taking it away. We're trying to get everybody on the same page and doing it. That's the key to winning—you have to take the ball away."

The staff meeting followed, a key trip to No. 18 Michigan State loomed, and Allen started on the state of players' minds.

"Some freshmen might be getting homesick," he said. "We didn't get a break in the middle of the season like we had planned where they could have gone home. Guys are fighting to get reps. Some of them are not where they want to be. That weighs on you. It plays with your mind."

He wanted each position coach to talk to his players.

"Focus on what you can control today, not tomorrow. Take a good step today, and then finish the week. Our key guys are in a good place. We've got to get reps and get the young guys up to speed." As for Michigan State, he added, "This is a great opportunity ahead of us. We've got to play our best."

Mounting injuries—the last thing IU needed—would force a change to the travel roster, which further boosted the need for player development. The Hoosiers were in a world of hurt. They had not been at full strength all season, starting by losing talented re-ceiver Nick Westbrook on the season-opening kickoff against Ohio State. This was a major problem given IU lacked the depth elite programs have. An injury to a frontline player was costlier than one to, say, Ohio State, which won the 2014 national championship with its *third-string* quarterback.

Injuries had rocked the offensive line and receiver positions. Among the injured was receiver Donavan Hale, who had beaten out Westbrook for a starting spot. If IU could have had Westbrook, Hale, and Simmie Cobbs together, it would have meant perhaps the nation's best receiving trio, which would have been a huge offensive boost.

Then there was the offensive line, which was already young and inexperienced. Injured right guard Simon Stepaniak didn't play against the Spartans. Starting left tackle Coy Cronk left the game in the second half with an injury. Tight end Ian Thomas was hurt and didn't play. Redshirt freshman Mackenzie Nworah, senior Danny Friend (a former tight end turned tackle), and junior Delroy Baker filled in.

"We have to make sure we get the right guys prepared," Allen said. "This is a critical game for us. Every guy matters."

This was Michigan State's homecoming game. The Spartans were seeking payback for IU's victory over them last season.

"They'll make a big deal about us beating them last year," Allen said.

For this game, both teams would be on the field for the playing of the National Anthem. Allen didn't want any of the player demonstrations—such as kneeling—that had surfaced in some NFL and college games happening on his team.

"I need to talk to the seniors. We'll be on the field for the National Anthem. We're not kneeling. We'll do it together. We'll be united. We're not taking a knee. No distractions."

⋆⇒◯◯⇐⋆

IU's takeaway emphasis paid off when Fields forced a fumble and defensive back Jonathan Crawford recovered at the Michigan State 15-yard line late in the first quarter, which resulted in Griffin Oakes's 33-yard field goal.

The Hoosier defense, led by linebacker Chris Covington and safety Chase Dutra, was outstanding. It held Michigan State to just 89 rushing yards and 274 total yards.

Covington had a career-high 11 tackles, including a sack. Dutra had a career-high 14 tackles.

IU allowed an 18-yard touchdown run by Michigan State's LJ Scott with less than two minutes remaining to put the Spartans ahead 17–9. The good news: IU offense had a chance to score a touchdown and 2-point conversion to get a tie and force overtime.

It was too much to ask.

IU lost by that 17–9 score.

Defenses ruled in the first half, which ended in a 3–3 tie. IU got Oakes's field goals of 44 yards in the third quarter and 20 yards in the fourth quarter for a 9–3 lead.

The Hoosiers could have—should have—scored a touchdown before Oakes's final field goal. A 12-play, 63-yard drive reached the Michigan State 2-yard line. Three straight runs went nowhere to lead to the field goal.

"We've got to score touchdowns," Allen said. "We know that and didn't do it."

The Spartans took the lead 10–9 late in the fourth quarter on Brian Lewerke's 10-yard touchdown pass to Felton Davis. The Hoosiers nearly forced a punt early in the drive, but on third and nineteen, Lewerke completed a 16-yard pass, which enabled Michigan State to successfully convert on fourth down and extend the drive.

Allen took the blame for the defensive call that led to Lewerke's crucial third-down completion.

"It's on me," Allen said. "That's going to really bother me."

Ramsey was solid in his first Big Ten road start. He completed 22 of 34 passes for 158 yards, no touchdowns, and no interceptions. He also rushed for 34 yards.

Punter Hayden Whitehead also had a big game. Four of his punts pinned Michigan State inside its 20-yard line. He averaged a career-best 43.6 yards.

In the end, it wasn't enough. For the second straight week, IU had positioned itself to upset a ranked team. For the second straight week, it couldn't come through. Opportunity lost.

"We didn't finish," Covington said. "We've got to finish. That's what we pride ourselves on. That was one of the breakthrough moments, and we didn't break through."

## CHAPTER 23

# Maryland

UNSTATED MUST-WIN-NOW PRESSURE WAS EVERYWHERE. Bowl hopes demanded it.

The 3–4 record wasn't good enough. Consecutive blown opportunities against ranked teams wasn't good enough. To make a bowl game, to reach the seven victories that would qualify as a breakthrough season, Indiana had to win four of its last five games. It *had* to beat a reeling Maryland team.

Allen pushed a fierce practice pace. On a cold, windy, gray day, he stalked the practice field with bullhorn intensity.

"It's full speed!" he shouted.

His focus was, as usual, on the defense. A play was run; the offense gained yards; the defense didn't play it correctly.

"We've got to see this," he shouted. "Read your keys!"

Moments later, after another play, when a linebacker was slow to the ball, Allen told linebackers coach William Inge, "He's got to come faster than that."

The Hoosiers drilled in thump mode, which meant they didn't tackle (as beat-up as the Hoosiers were, they didn't need overly physical practices), but they touched with emphasis. Allen wanted the defense focused on proper tackling form, which meant they had to position themselves as if they would be tackling.

"Finish! Finish! Sink the hips; tag from good position. Finish!"

And if they missed that point, safeties coach Noah Joseph added during the next play, "Finish it!" as linebacker Reakwon Jones intercepted a pass.

"That's it!" Allen shouted.

An hour or so later, coaches gathered in the War Room for a staff meeting. Allen was a man searching for answers that refused to come. The Hoosiers had to find a way. The opportunity was too great, the desired result too close, for them not to.

"Relentless is the word," he said. "Refuse to surrender."

The mood in the room was focused. Everyone knew the winning-record window was closing fast.

"We have to find creative ways," Allen said. "We had a good [practice] day. There was energy. I thought practice looked different in a good way. Not keeping them a long time Sunday helped."

He paused.

"A hunter is relentless in the pursuit of prey. That's the kind of team we have to have. Keep coming and coming. That's what we want."

He paused again. He considered injuries to defensive starters Marcelino Ball, A'Shon Riggins, and others.

"We have no depth on defense. That's the way it is. The number twos have to keep coming. That's the way it has to be."

Defeat could break the Hoosiers as it had so often in the past. Allen understood the threat of the here-we-go-again mind-set. You work so hard, come so close, only to fail again and again. IU had played four top-twenty teams—Ohio State, Penn State, Michigan, and Michigan State—and had a chance to win three of them. Only the Penn State game had been out of reach.

Allen had pushed to change the culture, and in so many ways—can you say defense?—he had. The Hoosiers were closer than they'd ever been to a program-changing victory. But losing can ruin everything if you let it. Allen had no intention of doing that. He wanted every player's best every day. A couple didn't deliver in the Tuesday practice, and it irritated him as few things could.

"I thought he played like a dog," Allen said about one player. "He was lazy in a negative way."

He said another player was, "Just as bad. That has to get fixed."

Allen's intensity was high because the stakes demanded it. Everyone knew this was a game—against a vulnerable, unranked opponent—the Hoosiers had to win.

"We have to persevere," Allen said about the injured players. "Do everything we can to get them back on the field."

He eyed his assistant coaches.

"If they're not buying in, it's on you."

The day after Michigan State heartbreak, eight days after Michigan overtime misery, six days before Maryland opportunity, he gathered the Hoosiers for a heart-to-heart chat.

"We had a good discussion as a team," Allen said. "It's very natural to get discouraged. Disappointed for sure and frustrated."

Allen said several Big Ten head coaches had contacted him about the Hoosiers' play—in a good way. "I didn't ask them. They chose to do that. They were complimentary of how hard we play, how well we've played, how physical we are, how tough our kids are. Just the way we've just battled and fought against really good football teams. They're impressed."

That was the setup. Then Allen delivered his key message.

"I told our guys, 'You can choose to feel sorry for yourselves, or you can realize you just played arguably the toughest schedule in the country to start the season and you're right there.' So you can get disappointed and hang your head and mope, or you can draw confidence from the way you performed.

"It's not how I told you that you could play but how you have physically shown to perform. You can draw strength and confidence from that and attack with more fervor and grit than ever before because you know you're right on the edge of breaking through."

IU was used to this kind of edge. They were 15–18 in their previous 33 games, with 10 of those losses by 10 or fewer points, three in overtime. Much of this came against some of the nation's best teams. In the Hoosiers' previous 29 games, they'd played nine top-ten teams and five top-five teams, fourteen ranked teams overall. Their first four 2017 losses against Ohio State, Penn State, Michigan, and Michigan State were a combined 24–4. All were ranked in the top twenty when the Hoosiers played them, with Ohio State and Penn State in the top five.

IU didn't need divine intervention to beat those teams. They just needed to make one or two more plays.

"It's a matter of staying the course and just not growing weary in the process," Allen said. "That's the key. That's our challenge as coaches. We've got five games left. How are we going to respond? How are we going to finish? So that word, 'finish,' applies to the game; it applies to a lot of things.

"It's a challenge to keep your mind right. I expect our guys to be highly energized and focused and locked in to play our best game. Our staff will lead by example. That's where we're at."

Five days later, the Hoosiers were at Maryland Stadium. A winning record likely depended on a victory.

The brutal schedule was about to turn not soft but manageable. Maryland had, like Indiana, a 3–4 record. It was playing its third-string quarterback after season-ending ACL injuries took out its two top, Tyrrell Pigrome and Kasim Hill. That left sophomore Max Bortenschlager, a former high school standout from Indianapolis—he'd led Cathedral High School to the 2014 Class 5A state title—who had picked up his play in the last three games with 6 touchdown passes and 1 interception.

Still, Bortenschlager had vulnerabilities—completing just 41 percent of his passes in the last three games—a good defense could exploit.

IU had a good defense.

In their previous three games, they had allowed 14.7 points, 81.0 passing yards, and 245.7 total yards. They ranked second nationally in forcing three and outs.

Maryland, meanwhile, had averaged just 16 points during their three-game losing streak. This was a game Indiana not only could win but had to win.

It did not.

The Hoosiers couldn't win even with Peyton Ramsey throwing for nearly 300 yards and three touchdowns in less than three quarters (an apparent knee injury knocked him out of the game), even with receivers Simmie Cobbs, Luke Timian, and Whop Philyor combing for 36 catches (the first time in school history three receivers had each caught at least 10 passes in a game) for 356 yards and 4 touchdowns, even with a defensive score on defensive end Allen Stallings's safety.

IU dominated time of possession (36 minutes to 23) and total yards (483 to 375) while converting an impressive 11 of 23 third-down opportunities and did that despite a seemingly never-ending series of injuries that now included leading rusher Morgan Ellison.

The Hoosiers still found a way to lose.

They allowed a blocked punt for a touchdown and had a blocked extra point. They gave up an 80-plus-yard kickoff return. With IU up 14–0 and in total control, Ramsey threw a terrible interception to set up Maryland's first touchdown. The defense couldn't force field goals to minimize the damage.

And then, trailing 42–39 in the final minute, with Richard Lagow at quarterback replacing the injured Ramsey, with the ball and a chance at victory, Philyor dropped a pass that would have produced a first down and kept the drive alive.

Yes, Philyor would win Big Ten freshman of the week for his 13-catch, 127-yard performance, but, still, a makeable play wasn't made.

Losses mounted.

Allen fumed.

"Just a really disappointing loss," he said in the aftermath. "Very disappointed with the way we played in special teams. That really let our team down and has been one of our strengths in many areas.

"To give up a blocked punt like we did at a critical time, to have an offensive turnover that led to their first score. We had a chance to get momentum and set the tone for the whole first quarter and did not do that.

"When you look at the big picture, you play really well offensively and did a lot of great things. Definitely a very strong performance to win the game on that side of the ball. Defensively played well across the board except for a couple big plays that we can't give up. Disappointed we gave those up. That ended up being the difference.

"But the long kickoff return, the blocked extra point, some kicks out of bounds, a short punt once, just multiple things in our special teams that we take a lot of pride in and was just unacceptable. You don't win on the road when you make those kind of mistakes."

IU's margin for error to have a breakthrough season now approached zero. It came down to this: beat No. 4 Wisconsin at Memorial Stadium and sweep through Illinois, Rutgers, and Purdue.

Anything less and breakthrough would become mediocrity—or worse.

## CHAPTER 24

# Wisconsin

THREE STRAIGHT LOSSES COULD BREAK THE HOOSIERS. Allen was determined not to let that happen. His staff meeting message to his coaches and, through them, the players was clear: the challenge was to serve, teach, and lead.

"Things haven't gone the way we wanted," he told the coaches. "Stay on your guys but have respect. Do your job of holding your guys accountable. When you lose, it ain't a lot of fun. It has to hurt. Fun is in the winning. If you want to feel differently, finish and win. Do the little things. Find a way to finish.

"There's a temptation to be discouraged. Don't fall into that trap. Stay the course. Continue to fight. Clench your fists and keep going. Fix what can be fixed."

Allen addressed the next practice. There was a chance of rain, and with all the injuries, the last thing IU needed was more of them because of a slick field.

"We'll go inside if it rains," Allen said. "I don't want to risk slips, groin and hamstring injuries."

As for the approach against unbeaten Wisconsin, Allen was clear: "I want to keep us in pressure mode. We have to attack on defense. Wisconsin is the number-four team. You don't get these opportunities every day."

A cynic could say the Hoosiers didn't need this kind of opportunity. Wisconsin had become a Hoosier nightmare. The Badgers had won nine straight meetings, the last four by margins of 48, 48, 52, and 63 points.

IU had no previous answer for Badger power, specifically a physical offensive line, a ruthless rushing attack, and a show-no-mercy approach. But these Hoosiers, even battered, seemed to have some answers. They'd been battle tested as Wisconsin hadn't. The Badgers' weak schedule featured zero ranked teams. The best opponent was a 5–3 Northwestern squad that reminded no one of, say, Penn State.

Allen had pushed a top-twenty-five defense goal all season. Based on Football Outsiders, a statistics website that keeps track of all sorts of stuff that is so complicated not even geeks understand them, Allen had a top-twenty-five defense. Created by Brian Fremeau and Bill Connelly, two really smart guys who love math, Football Outsiders tracked every possession and every play in every game, looking for key factors such as efficiency, explosiveness, field position, finishing drives, and turnovers. Add it all up and IU had a top-twenty-five defense on standard downs and an elite defense on obvious passing situations. That meant it matched up well with Wisconsin, which ran 75 percent of the time on first and second downs and which led the Big Ten in rushing at 245.8 yards a game.

Plus, Badger superstar freshman tailback Jonathan Taylor was banged up.

"You have to have different personnel groups to match that style," Allen said. "This is the biggest, strongest, and most physical offense we've faced. They have a heavy emphasis on running. It's completely different than what we faced at Maryland."

Beyond that, Wisconsin featured a stifling defense that ranked fifth nationally in points allowed (12.9) and fifth in total defense (268.0 yards allowed). The Badgers led the nation in passing efficiency defense, which measured opponents' completion percentage, yards per pass attempt, passing touchdowns allowed, and interceptions. They led the conference in sacks, with 27.

No matter. The Hoosiers needed a win in the worst way, and for the game's first sixteen minutes, they dominated.

Richard Lagow threw a 23-yard touchdown pass to running back Devonte Williams near the end of the first quarter. Griffin Oakes kicked a field goal early in the second quarter. Indiana led 10–0 and had the momentum.

Wisconsin countered by scoring the next 24 points. Then Lagow connected with Simmie Cobbs on an 18-yard TD pass to cut the Badgers lead to 7, at 24–17, entering the fourth quarter.

Wisconsin owned the fourth quarter by a 21–0 score—intercepting a pair of Lagow passes was a big factor—to turn a close game into a blowout win.

Lagow was 20 for 34 for 226 yards and 2 touchdowns and those 2 late interceptions.

"It's going to be 'look in the mirror' a little bit," Lagow said in the aftermath. "Costly penalties. Turnovers. It wasn't so much what they were doing on defense but rather us shooting ourselves in the foot.

"Football is a hard game. Stuff happens. Everybody is out there trying their absolute hardest to win every Saturday."

Allen was more to the point after seeing the statistics that showed Wisconsin had a 237- to 40-yard rushing edge, a 407 to 255 total yard advantage, and a 3 to 1 turnover edge.

"It's about protecting the football and creating takeaways," Allen said. "We played a great football team, but when you're minus in the takeaway ratio, you're not going to win. We didn't run the football well enough. That's for sure. We didn't stop the run well enough, for sure. But for me, it was all about takeaways."

IU's record dropped to 3–6. It needed to sweep its final three opponents—Illinois, Rutgers, and Purdue—to make a third straight bowl game.

"I feel good about getting our guys in the right mind-set," Allen said in the postgame press conference. "We've just got to physically get ourselves healed up so we can have a strong finish. It's definitely a tough mental battle you find yourself in.

"Sometimes life is not fair. Sometimes things happen, but you've got to learn to really fight through as a man, as a leader. So I think it's a great precursor to their future.

"We're going to teach them about life. And I believe they're going to finish really well. I think this team will be remembered as a team that played a very, very difficult schedule but finished well."

Before that, in the locker room right after the game, Allen was more passionate while talking to his team.

"I want everyone to listen very carefully. It's a pretty simple game, isn't it? Get fumbles. Ball is on the ground, and we don't get the ball. We turn the ball over, and they go score. We turn it over again, they score. All three of their [fourth-quarter] touchdowns came from our turnovers. That's the key. Do you understand?"

"Yes, sir," the players said.

"We get a pick in the end zone, and we don't score. See the difference? It's about protecting the football and getting the football from them! That's the reality. This is where we're at.

"That's a top-five team in the country. If you don't turn the ball over, what happens? It's right there. Neck and neck. Right there. That's what it comes down to. Protecting the ball or not protecting the ball. Take if from them or not take it from them. That's the name of the game. That's why we make such a big deal about takeaways on defense and turnovers on offense.

"Here's the truth. You got a choice to make. We have three opportunities left. All that matters is the next one. You get to decide how this will finish. Seniors, you get to decide how this will finish. I want everyone in this room who is not playing because they're injured to do everything possible to get back on the field and help this team. Is that clear?"

"Yes, sir," the players said.

"Everything you can do! If you can't, you can't, but I want everything you can do to help this team finish strong. I promise you that's what you're going to get from me. That's what you'll get from me! We're going to finish, men.

"Out there wasn't good enough. We didn't protect the ball. We didn't create takeaways. Period. I'm not dwelling on this game. I refuse to look backwards. Look [in] one direction—that's straight ahead. Earmuffs and blinders! Is that clear?"

"Yes, sir."

"That's the bottom line. That's what this is all about.

"Seniors, you have three more opportunities. You just played a really good team. When you don't protect the ball, that's what happens. When you don't get takeaways, that's what happens.

"I care about the men in this room. We're going to fight and compete together, period. Make wise choices; take care of yourselves. We'll come back tomorrow. Bring it up! It's about family, men. It's about doing it together.

"L-E-O!"

CHAPTER 25

# Rutgers

THE MEMORIAL STADIUM LOCKER ROOM WAS ROCKING. The momentum from the Illinois victory the previous week had carried over to a second straight win, this time over Rutgers in the home finale, and the postgame locker room was packed—with the usual players and coaches, plus staff, families, friends, and loved ones. This was a time to celebrate and share.

"I'm so proud of how you guys stayed together," coach Tom Allen shouted in a hoarse voice in the aftermath of the must-win 41–0 victory over Rutgers. "Seniors, you deserved that."

The team erupted into applause and cheers.

"It's the first Big Ten shutout since 1993, baby!" Allen shouted.

More cheers.

"It's the largest margin of victory since 1990!"

Even more cheers.

"Take care of your teammates tonight. Be great teammates and do things to help this program finish strong. We know what we have to do now."

He paused.

"It is officially Purdue week."

IU would end their regular season at rival Purdue the next Saturday in what loomed as a one-game playoff for a bowl bid. Both teams were 5–6. The winner would be bowl eligible. The loser would spend the holidays at home.

"Yeah, baby," a player shouted.

"When you talk to media, you're always respectful," Allen shouted. "Take the high road. Do you understand me?"

"Yes, sir."

"Let's keep our mouths shut, work our tails off, and we finish," Allen shouted. "We finish, men!"

Against Rutgers, a team with its own bowl aspirations with a 4–6 record, Indiana finished as never before in its most complete game of the season.

Not even a nearly two-hour second-half weather delay—players spent much of the time watching other college football games—could diminish the quality of IU's play.

"What I love was that we started strong and finished strong," Allen said.

The result was Indiana's most lopsided Big Ten victory since a 42–0 win at Northwestern in 1990 and their first Big Ten shutout since beating Michigan State 10–0 in 1993. Add October's 27–0 win over Charleston Southern, and it's the first time IU had recorded two shutouts in the same season since 1993.

Over the previous two games, Indiana allowed just 14 total points while totaling 12 sacks and forcing 6 takeaways. Beyond that, it was a day to honor the seniors—and celebrate the fiftieth anniversary of IU's only Rose Bowl appearance.

"We went out there and gave it our all," senior defensive end Greg Gooch said. "We were going to leave it all out at Memorial Stadium."

The Hoosiers, who were a defensive disaster before Allen arrived a year and a half earlier, delivered big time.

"A shutout is hard to do," Allen said in the postgame press conference. "That's pretty special. It's very fitting.

"When I got here, they had lost some confidence. They had some soul searching to do. I appreciate they stayed with us."

IU turned Rutgers's offense—already the Big Ten's second worst—into irrelevance. The Scarlet Knights managed just 190 total yards and 11 first downs. They punted nine times.

"They play hard," Rutgers's Chris Ash said of IU. "They play with good fundamentals."

Offensively, the Hoosiers found their running game—and just about everything else. They rushed for a season-high 271 yards. Tailback Morgan's Ellison's 149 rushing yards would earn him his second Big Ten freshman-of-the-week award. Cole Gest added 104 yards in the first 100-yard effort of his career. Offensive lineman Brandon Knight had a huge blocking performance.

Beyond that, the offensive line didn't allow a sack and didn't commit a false start or a holding penalty. It reflected the strong work of offensive line coach Darren Hiller and a group of young linemen growing into their roles.

Offensive coordinator Mike DeBord said he'd never seen that kind of performance.

"Usually you have something in there," he said. "It was great focus by our players. One day we practiced outside in miserable weather. When you have to concentrate in practice and the conditions are the same in the game, it's a bonus. Sometimes teams go inside in weather like that, but we stayed outside. That helped in preparation."

As a result, Hoosier coaches awarded the entire line—Coy Cronk, Mackenzie Nworah, Wes Martin, Hunter Littlejohn, Knight, and Delroy Baker—as offensive players of the game.

"I'm really proud of their performance," Allen said. "They still have things to continue to work on, but . . . it was a great job."

Quarterback Richard Lagow threw for 236 yards and 2 touchdowns. It could have been more, but the Hoosiers stopped passing in the third quarter. They ended the game with 27 straight runs that produced 2 touchdowns.

"They whipped us up front on both sides of the ball, and the result is what it is," Ash said. "We didn't play well, and that's on me."

Two weeks earlier, IU had been floundering with a 3–6 record and four straight losses. Now they had a chance to make a third straight bowl for the first time since the late 1980s and just the second time in program history.

"It means a lot," Allen said. "We made it through all those tough times. We have an opportunity to do something very special here. We're still building the culture and the program. To withstand all that and say it comes down to one game is very rewarding."

So was the play of Lagow, who had thrived since returning to a starting role after Peyton Ramsey's injury in late October.

"It's Rich's poise and confidence," Allen said. "He's responded exactly like you'd want him to. He handled adversity like a man. He's being rewarded for being a quality person."

As far as the game, a fierce wind—steady in the 30-mph range with gusts up to 58 mph—contributed to Rutgers's early fumbled punt return. The Hoosiers' Rashard Fant recovered, and Ellison ran it in from the 6-yard line on the next play. IU led 7–0.

The Hoosiers took advantage of having the wind at their backs— and busted Rutgers's pass coverage—when Lagow hit tight end Ian Thomas for a 57-yard touchdown.

The Hoosiers added field goals of 26 and 20 yards from Griffin Oakes for a 20–0 halftime lead.

IU didn't slow down in the second half. It got third-quarter touchdowns from receiver Luke Timian (a 19-yard pass from Lagow) and a 1-yard Ellison run set up by Ellison's 45-yard run. That made it 34–0 before the weather delay hit. Add an 8-yard touchdown run midway through the fourth quarter to complete the scoring.

Now it came down to Purdue, and the stakes couldn't be higher. The Boilers were 5–6 after a stunning win at Iowa, the same Hawkeyes who had crushed powerhouse Ohio State at Kinnick Stadium a few weeks earlier.

So the Oaken Bucket Game would be a winner-take-all showdown, which was fine with Allen. "We understand the magnitude of the game," he said. "This has nothing to do with the records. We're playing for a ton of pride and who you represent. It will be a tremendous challenge for us. You don't want distractions of the week to overwhelm you.

"There's one last key game to be played."

CHAPTER 26

# Purdue

THE PURDUE BOILERMAKERS LOOMED, AND TOM ALLEN
seethed in the Tuesday staff meeting. He sat at the end of the War
Room table radiating energy. He wasn't excited about the just-com-
pleted Tuesday practice, and he wasn't alone.

"It thought it was just OK," defensive line coach Mark Hagen
said. "It looked like a bunch of sore guys."

A player had gotten on Allen's wrong side, which meant he hadn't
practiced with passion and commitment—and it wasn't the first
time. Allen seethed some more.

"He acted like he was eighty years old," Allen said. "I didn't look
at him or talk to him or give him any sympathy."

Purdue week had finally arrived, bringing rivalry tension and
energy few other programs could match, and if it lacked the national
implications of Ohio State-Michigan or Alabama-Auburn, never
underestimate passion.

Beyond that were the bowl implications. Win, and a third straight
bowl bid was assured. That had happened just once before in IU
history—from 1986–1988. Lose, and . . . well, nobody was planning
for that.

"We've got to fight for everything," Allen said. "We have an opportunity at our fingertips."

Allen wanted to ensure players were ready.

"What can we do to get their bodies OK?" he asked, then answered his own question.

"Make sure your guys who need it are doing it," he told his coaches. "That they're getting extra catches or stretches or massages or whatever it is. Make sure your guys get what they need."

He paused.

"I like the focus of our older guys. It will take all of us."

Another pause.

"I didn't think it was our best practice."

It wasn't all negative. Offensive coordinator Mike DeBord liked the offensive starters' practice energy. Allen listened and jotted down notes. The dominating Rutgers win popped into consideration.

"Our guys should feel good about themselves," Allen said. "They just played the most complete game here in a while. What you get, you earn. We played that way because of the way we prepared. That's where leadership comes in."

He paused yet again, this time from the memory of the disappointing loss at Maryland. IU would already be bowl eligible if they had won that game.

"Maryland helps a lot," he said. "We didn't prepare the right way, and it cost us."

Then there were the heartbreaking losses to nationally ranked Michigan and Michigan State.

"There's no question we let Michigan and Michigan State off the hook, no question that we blew it at Maryland," Allen said.

He eyed the men in the room.

"But we finish this week off right, and everything changes."

IU had hosted the previous two Oaken Bucket games and three of the last four, a big reason why it had won four straight in the series for the first time since the late 1940s. They had never won five in a row over the Boilers.

This time the game was at Purdue's Ross-Ade Stadium. The winner-gets-a-bowl-loser-goes-home stakes had generated sellout energy. More than fifty-two thousand would show up.

"They're frothing at the mouth," Allen said of the Boilers. "It will be a great atmosphere. The way it's supposed to be."

The game had lost statewide zest in the previous few years, partly due to IU not having had a winning season since 2007, mostly the consequence of Purdue's freefall under former head coach Darrell Hazell (just nine wins in four seasons). Offensive guru Jeff Brohm had been hired from Western Kentucky and had made instant impact.

Zest was back, and Allen's eyes showed it.

"I was so disappointed about the last few years with the energy in the series," he said. "Now it's back to being at a fever pitch. That's what you want. Purdue is [ticked] off. They'll run their mouths. It will be that way—the way it's supposed to be. That's what I'm used to.

"It ain't going to be civil. It will be nasty. Be ready for a fistfight for sixty minutes. That's how I see it. Embrace it and get your guys ready to play."

No Hoosier would be readier than backup tight end Ryan Watercutter, a full-throttle junior seeing the first significant action of his career. He was banged up and didn't care. He wanted a piece of the Boilers.

"I think you'd have to remove Watercutter's arm for him not to play," Allen said. "He's who you want fighting in this game."

Allen paused. He was ready for kickoff.

"However much fight they bring, we'll double it," he said. "I promise you that."

---

Promise crashed against Bucket Game reality. Purdue under Brohm had returned to postseason relevance. Indiana had not.

It showed early. The Boilers played with offensive balance and defensive tenacity to bolt to leads of 21–7 and 31–10. IU rallied to within 7 points with a minute remaining and needed a second successful on-side kick (Chase Dutra had recovered the first one) for a chance to force overtime.

It didn't happen.

So there was Allen, fresh off the 31–24 defeat, pushing for perspective amid bitter disappointment. He gathered players and staff in the tiny Ross-Ade Stadium visiting locker room, the same locker room Michigan coach Jim Harbaugh had ripped a month earlier for its lack of charm and functionality. These were young men who had meant so much to Allen, who had done everything he'd asked, who had pushed so hard for so long.

The breakthrough-season goal was over. A third straight bowl appearance wouldn't happen. A 5–7 record wasn't good enough.

Allen stood in front of this team one last time in a postgame setting, voice hoarse, brow damp, eyes red. He demanded that no one blame or point fingers, that everyone handle the situation with class. He pushed the message that had been a constant through all the ups and down: L-E-O.

"I told them to make sure they do a great job in the classroom, of being pros," Allen said in the postgame press conference. "Our job is to help them become the men they are supposed to be. That's important to me.

"Make sure the seniors finish well. The young guys have to get their bodies rested and ready to go. We have a very important off-season ahead of us."

There would be no next IU season for seniors such as Richard Lagow, Tegray Scales, and Chase Dutra. You'd better believe it hurt.

"I really wanted another month with the guys on this team," Lagow said. "That's the most disappointing thing."

Everything ends, of course, but the preference was to end on a bowl-victory high rather than a rivalry-loss low. Preference crashed amid penalties, breakdowns, and a season-long inability to make the difference-making play.

"I wanted to go to the bowl game," Dutra said. "I wanted to win the Bucket again. You want to go out at the highest level possible. To lose to [Purdue], it just hurts. You wish you didn't have these moments."

A pause.

"It's life."

It was a season of near misses, with heartbreaking losses to Michigan in overtime, then at Michigan State and Maryland.

"That's how it's been the last couple of seasons," Dutra said. "We let some get away. You say, 'What if?'"

But it will be better, he added. "This senior class set a strong foundation. The guys below us know what to expect. They know the expectations. We'll get there."

On Saturday, with so much at stake, in a game that demanded full-throttle execution, the Hoosiers misfired. That's a shame.

"We weren't ready," Allen said. "That's on me. This is disappointing. I expected us to be going to a bowl game. To come up one game short isn't what I wanted. There's no question nobody played more top teams than we did. That's a fact. That's part of it. You have to find a way to win enough games and extend your season."

Purdue attacked Lagow nearly nonstop, pressuring and punishing and often leaving him little time to let plays fully develop. Still, he threw 60 passes and completed 32 for 373 yards and 3 touchdowns.

In ten games, Lagow threw for 1,936 yards, 15 touchdowns, and 8 interceptions. IU's defense, which had been so strong the previous two weeks in allowing just 14 total points, faded in the final 35 minutes against a Markell Jones–led rushing onslaught. Jones finished with 217 yards, which is close to what he had entering the game (263).

What went wrong?

"Markel is a great player," Scales said. "He ran well. They have a great offensive line, great coaching."

A first-quarter 7–7 draw offered Hoosier hope. A 14–0 Boiler burst near the end of the second quarter—including a 22-yard pass off a fake punt—negated some of it.

Enter Ricky Brookins.

IU's backup tailback delivered a 64-yard run, the longest of his career, to set up the potential for a momentum-shifting touchdown at the Purdue 11-yard line. Brookins added seven more yards on a catch, but that was as far as the drive went.

IU settled for Griffin Oakes's 22-yard field goal and a 21–10 score. Momentum was muted but not gone.

Then came a Lagow-to-Simmie Cobbs Jr. third-quarter touchdown that wasn't, wiped out by a chop-block penalty on offensive lineman Mackenzie Nworah. Still, the deficit was just 11 at 21–10. Everything was there for the Hoosiers if they dared take it.

They dared.

They couldn't take.

"This year didn't turn out the way we wanted," Lagow said, "but you look at the games we lost, it's close. You can see how close it is."

Close included the top-25 defense goal. IU ended the regular season at No. 26 in total defense, allowing 340.1 yards a game. Boise State was No. 25, allowing 339.0. In looking at the 2018 season, IU would have to replace key seniors from that defense: cornerback Rashard Fant; safeties Chase Dutra and Tony Fields; Scales; linebacker Chris Covington; defensive tackle Nate Hoff; and defensive ends Greg Gooch and Robert McCray.

Even amid defeat, the future was very much on Allen's mind. The next day, he and his staff hit the recruiting road and basically stayed away from home for the next three weeks. The new early signing period—December 20–22—loomed with growing urgency.

"It's time to evaluate," Allen said. "We lose some quality guys. The signing class will be big. We need more depth. We've got to roll more guys in, develop more guys, get guys stronger. That's the number-one priority. We continue that process [with recruiting]. From top to bottom, evaluate everything we do to make sure we're doing everything possible to play at a high level."

Allen will take the Hoosiers to that level, Lagow said.

"He's the guy for the job. There isn't any doubt about it."

IU hoped 5–7 disappointment would breed new opportunity . . . and more bowls. If it does, when it does, it will come from Allen's program cornerstone: L-E-O. Love each other.

CHAPTER 27

# Final Thoughts

TOM ALLEN RECLINED ON A COUCH IN HIS SPACIOUS
Memorial Stadium office, tie missing but at the ready, pumped for
a December 2017 alumni event at Henke Hall to recognize the 2018
signing class, perhaps the best recruiting group in program history.

It helped soothe the sting from missed bowl opportunity.

Most recruiting services rated IU's 2018 class in the top forty
nationally but No. 6 in the rugged six-team Big Ten East, which
reflected the annual challenge the Hoosiers face.

No matter. Allen was eager to embrace the future and contemplate a head coaching debut season that, with a final 5–7 record,
hadn't delivered on its breakthrough hopes.

"The frustration is still there," he said, a couple of weeks removed
from the season's end. "I still feel it. The disappointment. I expected
us to win more than we did."

Indiana could easily have won seven games. That it did not, that
it lost the rivalry opportunity to Purdue with the postseason on the
line, frustrated and motivated.

"That's what left such a bad taste after the Purdue game," Allen said. "We knew we were so close. We'd been close before, but
this was different. There were a lot of positives. So many things
we continue to advance, but there are things we need to address.
For whatever reason, we haven't finished well—whether it's better
strength and conditioning, better depth, execution. We'll continue
to address that."

That process became clearer a few days later, when Allen decided to part with strength coach Keith Caton, who had been hired by former head coach Kevin Wilson. Caton spent the 2016 and '17 seasons with the Hoosiers after a four-year run at Baylor.

"I would like to thank Keith Caton for his service to Indiana University and to our football program over the last two years," Allen said in a statement. "I have a lot of respect for him as a husband and a father. Keith is a tremendous person, and I wish him nothing but the very best moving forward."

Allen replaced Caton with former Indiana fullback David Ballou, who had spent the previous season as Notre Dame's co-director of football strength and conditioning. Ballou also spent fourteen years as the head strength and conditioning coach at Avon High School near Indianapolis. Avon won six state titles in multiple sports during his time there.

Allen also hired Dr. Matt Rhea from IMG Academy in Florida as athletic performance coach. A prime objective was improving team speed.

"David Ballou is one of the more highly respected strength coaches in the country," Allen said in a university release. "I have known him for many years and have followed his work at both the high school and collegiate levels. We are looking forward to him working with our program and helping us achieve our goals on and off the field."

Another top priority was quarterback. Richard Lagow and Peyton Ramsey had alternated strong play with struggles. Winning teams don't have that inconsistency as such a crucial position. Strong, reliable quarterback play had to be developed. With Lagow graduating, it would fall first to Ramsey, although Allen would bring in quarterbacks to challenge him in freshman Michael Penix Jr. and Arizona graduate transfer Brandon Dawkins.

"That hurt us," Allen said about the quarterback play. "I know we were that one component away from being a really good team. Our defense finished top twenty-six. We wanted to be top twenty-five and missed it by one spot. We had six categories where we were a top-twenty-five defense. We have changed that culture. We have to have all three phases—defense, offense, special teams—to create those end-of-game situations we want."

As far as the season, Allen said, "There was a lot of excitement building up. You're in your first year, just a lot of anxiety with the unknown in that role of [defensive coordinator] and head coach. Trying to manage everything going on.

"Then there was so much buildup to the Ohio State game. You think about how that game went. I asked our guys at the end of the season what was the breakthrough for our team. Many said they felt it was the first three quarters of that game. That was the way we envisioned us playing. You saw what we could become.

"It was the reality of not being able to maintain it at the end. It was a forecast of some of our issues—lack of depth, lack of our ability to finish. At the same time, it was one of the first times in a long time we had a situation like that.

"We're beating them at the end of the first quarter. We're beating them at halftime. We go up 21–20 late in the third quarter.

"It had a whole different feel to it. We were different."

A pause.

"We couldn't maintain it at the end."

That was true so often in 2017. IU lost four games by 8 points or less, one in overtime.

"We've got to find a way to win those close games," Allen said. "We had chances to beat top-twenty teams. That's the next thing we want so bad."

The goal was to turn wanting into doing. Allen insisted it wasn't a matter of *if* but *when*.

"There is a consistent expectation that we compete at a high level every time we take the field. There's not a drop-off. We have to be consistent every week. We've been that way. There is enough young talent that they got a chance to experience that. They also got a chance to experience the devastation of being close. The more guys want to change it, the more it intensifies their passion to make that change."

Again, he insisted, change was coming.

"We have a great signing class. We've got to keep building. We've got to stay the course. Keep true to who you are and what you believe. That's why this season was a great learning situation for me.

"The big lesson goes back to the value of the depth we have to have. When injuries start to mount, we don't have the next guy in at the same level, or we have players on defense taking too many snaps, especially at linebacker and the secondary. That comes back to bite you.

"We have to keep recruiting at a high level. We've got to improve our strength and conditioning, and we've got to continue to develop the guys we have.

"Another big lesson was managing the game. In the beginning, when the defense came off the field, it was hard for me to focus on the defensive adjustments because I was thinking about the offense."

Allen pointed to recruiting as the ultimate difference maker.

"It's the way we're recruiting. It's putting one good class, then another good class, then another good class. That's how you have to create the depth we need to compete.

"The optimism is from seeing a product on the field that is getting to the point where we envision it to be. It's not where we want it to be, but we're making progress. That encourages more passion and focus to close the gap."

You might have thought the Purdue loss would have hurt Hoosier recruiting. You would have been wrong.

"Coming off the loss to Purdue," Allen said, "I was shocked at how positive everyone was. Every school I went to, every home I visited, people looked at us differently. There was a lot of optimism. They love how hard our kids play. They love the intensity and passion they play with. Each week it was never different. That sends a message. Something good is happening, and as a recruit, I want to help you break through. You're fun to watch."

As far as the December 20 signing day, IU landed twenty-three prospects, including standouts such as Penix, a four-star (out of five) quarterback out of Florida and Indiana Mr. Football Reese Taylor out of Indianapolis Ben Davis.

Allen said, "When the day starts, you're exhausted, but you leave energized because of what just happened. When it all is done, you crash. You've just been going and going and going. You just finish a long season, and the very next day you're on a plane flying somewhere, and that hasn't stopped. It eventually takes its toll. You go off adrenaline."

The adrenaline resulted in IU meeting its recruiting needs at offensive line, defensive line, secondary, quarterback, and linebacker. That included getting offensive lineman Nick Linder, a graduate transfer from the University of Miami. He had one year of eligibility and could play immediately.

As far as the class's strong national ranking, Allen said, "What do these young men develop into? That's the question. What do these guys look like two years from now, three years from now?

"You get fired up about rankings. This is a great class. I don't focus on that. It's 'what do these guys become?'"

Allen's wife, Tracy, briefly entered the room. She was helping with the celebration preparations as she did with so many things while balancing her own successful educational consulting business. She and her husband are, in every way, a team.

The time to head to the reception was nearing, but Allen wasn't close to ending his thoughts on the state of the Hoosiers. He insisted they're on the verge of sustained success to rival that of former coach Bill Mallory.

A glowing Memorial Stadium lit up the night as if to emphasize that.

"I do see us having that kind of success," Allen said. "Once again, it's knowing who you are, knowing what you want and not let anybody talk you out of it.

"I've talked to a lot of coaches. So many said, 'We love what you're doing. Don't change. Keep doing what you're doing. Keep fighting.

Don't let the scoreboard or the won-loss record deter you from the course you're on.'

"Coach Mallory is the one who did it. He built it. It took a certain period of time. He built it in a certain way that they had consistent performances. They were consistently competing to be in the late-season hunt for the Big Ten and bowl games. That's what I want. I want us to be in the hunt. I want us to be competing. We are competing. You've got those two to three games we're not winning. I talked to [Northwestern] coach Pat Fitzgerald. They were 9–3 and inches away from being 3–9.

"I believe in our core principles. I believe we're doing everything we can do to have success."

Behind him are the signs of what those principles can produce and what the program means. There's a plaque for Allen being nominated for the 2016 Broyles Award, which goes annually to the nation's best assistant coach. There's a photo of Allen touching Hep's Rock in a tribute to former coach Terry Hoeppner. There are books that reflect the man and his beliefs: *The Edge*, *Beyond the Game*, *The Coach's Bible*, and *Today's Moment of Truth*.

Finally, there is the framed photo of a lion, a gift from Tracy and her belief that her husband is the Lion Chaser because of his bravery, focus, and determination. It reflected, as nothing else could, that success is coming.

In so many ways, it is already here.

# References

Indiana University Football 2017 Record Book

Indiana University Weekly Game Notes

IUHoosiers.com (IU's Athletic Department website)

Holiday Bowl quotes: Robinson, Doug. "1979 Holiday Bowl: Indiana 38, BYU 37. Whoosiers? Surprise Cougars, as BYU's Bowl Jinx Still Alive." *Deseret News*, December 22, 1979. https://www.deseretnews.com /article/230012399/1979-Holiday-Bowl-Indiana-38-BYU-37.html.

My notes and quotes acquired while covering and attending IU practices, meetings, press conferences, and games during the 2017 season.

Interviews with Tom Allen, Tom Allen Sr., Janet Allen, Tracy Allen, Thomas Allen, Fred Glass, Bill Mallory, Kate Miller, Don Fischer, Bob Hammel, Ken Kaczmarek, Eric Stolberg, Lee Corso, Reece Davis, Dick Dullaghan, Richard Lagow, Tegray Scales, Peyton Ramsey, Simmie Cobbs, Rashard Fant, Tony Fields, Mark Hagen, and Noah Joseph (Interviews were conducted between February 2017 and December 2017.)

**Pete DiPrimio** is an award-winning sports writer, a long-time author and freelance writer, and a member of the Indiana Sportswriters and Sports Broadcasters Hall of Fame. He's also a recruiter and special projects writer for National Salvage & Service Corporation. He's been an adjunct lecturer for the National Sports Journalism Center at IUPU–Indianapolis and for Indiana University's School of Journalism. He is the author of three nonfiction books (two on basketball, one on baseball) pertaining to Indiana University athletics, a co-author with John Decker of another book on IU athletics (*Unknown, Untold, and Unbelievable Stories of IU Sports*) through IU Press, and more than two dozen children's books. He is seeking an agent for his first novel, a sports thriller. Pete is also a fitness instructor, plus a tennis, racquetball, biking, and weightlifting enthusiast.